INFORMED

UNTANGLING DESTRUCTIVE INTERPRETATIONS OF SCRIPTURE

Other Books by Douglas Jacoby

A Quick Overview of the Bible

Answering Skeptics

Campus Core

Compelling Evidence for God and the Bible

Exodus: Night of Redemption

Jesus and Islam

Life to the Full: James, Peter, John, Jude

Origins (Genesis 1–11)

Principle-Centered Parenting

The Lion Roared: An Exposition of Amos

The Radical Life of Elijah: Chariots of Fire

The Spirit

The Ultimate Bible Quiz Book

Thrive! Using Psalms to Help You Flourish

Till the Nets Are Full

What Happens After We Die?

What's the Truth about Heaven and Hell?

When God Is Silent

INFORMED

UNTANGLING DESTRUCTIVE INTERPRETATIONS OF SCRIPTURE

DOUGLAS JACOBY AND JOSEPH HARRIS

INFORMED

Untangling Destructive Interpretations of Scripture

ISBN: 978-1-948450-32-4. Printed in the United States of America.

Interior book design: Toney C. Mulhollan.

Cover design: Roy Applesamy.

Illumination Publishers titles may be purchased in bulk for classroom instruction, business, fund-raising, or sales promotional use. For information, please email paul.ipibooks@me.com.

Illumination Publishers cares deeply about using renewable resources and uses recycled paper whenever possible.

The views expressed by the authors are their own and do not necessarily reflect the views of Illumination Publishers.

Published by Illumination Publishers, 6010 Pinecreek Ridge Court, Spring, Texas 77379-2513. www.ipibooks.com.

ILLUMINATION PUBLISHERS

About the authors: Since 2003, **Douglas Jacoby** has been a freelance teacher and consultant. With degrees from Duke, Harvard, and Drew, he has written more than thirty books, recorded over 750 podcasts, and spoken in 125 nations around the world. Douglas is also professor of theology at Lincoln Christian University. In *Informed,* he digs deep to share both biblically and personally from his first four decades as a follower of Christ. For more about the work and ministry of Douglas Jacoby go to www.douglasjacoby.com.

Joseph Harris is a husband, father, author, teacher, and speaker specializing in helping people to understand the Bible and experience deeper love by living according to the teachings of Jesus.

Joseph holds degrees from Princeton University and the University of Phoenix and has also done additional academic work at Princeton University, Princeton Theological Seminary, University of Pennsylvania, Montclair State University, Trinity Theological Seminary, Columbia Biblical Seminary, and the Rocky Mountain School of Ministry and Theology.

Joseph has an international teaching and speaking ministry called Teach Me the Bible. He is also the codirector of the Athens Institute of Ministry (www.athensinstitute.org), which teaches courses in biblical and religious studies online and in various locations internationally.

Table of Contents

Table of Contents

The Beginning and the End

Informed is a book about truth and error; in particular, it is about how thoughtful readers of the Bible can navigate the multiplicity of human teachings claiming to be biblical (Colossians 2:8). Many of these teachings are destructive. Others simply skew the gospel message. As with the labyrinth of ancient mythology, finding our way can be confusing, to say the least.

It would be easy for some readers to conclude that Harris and Jacoby are presenting themselves as the final interpreters and evaluators of the various doctrines we are critiquing. Let us emphasize that we are still on the journey—we have not arrived—and are open to input. (That is, we hope to hear from you.) Besides that, having it all together doctrinally, if such a thing is even possible, can hardly be the prime criterion for salvation. We agree that "Christianity had plenty of chinks in its doctrinal armor in the early days, when its creeds were still solidifying, and state-sponsored persecution was buffeting it on all sides."[1]

While many readers will prefer to read straight through, others may prefer to consult *Informed* as a handbook. Either way, we hope you won't skip to the most relevant parts without reading the opening and closing chapters. That is because Chapters 1 and 14 contain ideas and perspectives that are critical to our thinking. As many readers will soon realize, we are attempting to shift the way Christians think about doctrine. We believe that most Bible readers—ourselves included—have for too long approached the Bible with false assumptions. We have relied on it as a book of truths, regulations, and doctrines. We have made the Bible into a legal text, instead of a disclosure of the heart of God. This needs to change.

So please begin with the beginning. (And end with the end.)

—Douglas Jacoby and Joseph Harris

1

Doctrine – It's Not What We Think

The word "doctrine" simply means teaching, that is, the content of what one teaches—as when we refer to "the teaching of Jesus" (e.g., Matthew 5–7). In contrast to this, most tend to think of doctrine as a set of religious tenets or denominational dogmas, often technically written up. However, in the Bible, doctrine entails behaviors more than beliefs. We know this because, when we are asked to speak on the subject of sound doctrine, people usually expect a talk on biblical baptism versus the Sinner's Prayer, the first-century gift of tongues, or marrying only committed Christians—issues that define a fellowship.[2] True, all of these matters are illuminated by careful Bible study. But is this how the writers of the New Testament normally understood "sound doctrine"? Let's see how the apostle Paul approached the matter.

We know that the law is good if one uses it properly. We also know that the law is made not for the righteous but for lawbreakers and rebels, the ungodly and sinful,

> *the unholy and irreligious, for those who kill their fathers or mothers, for murderers, for the sexually immoral, for those practicing homosexuality, for slave traders and liars and perjurers—and for whatever else is* ***contrary to the sound doctrine*** *that conforms to the gospel concerning the glory of the blessed God, which he entrusted to me* (1 Timothy 1:8–11, emphasis added).

What sorts of things are "contrary" to sound doctrine? Misunderstanding the workings of the Holy Spirit? Confusion about the relationship between divine sovereignty and free will? Look again at the Scripture citation above. *None* of the items in Paul's list are what most Christians would consider doctrinal matters. But they were doctrinal matters to Paul. They include things like:

- The slave trade
- Lying
- Homosexuality
- Rebellion
- Murder

It may be difficult to see how such actions or practices are *theological* errors. But think about it. A rebel typically does not submit to human authority—let alone divine authority. A murderer usurps God's right to give and take away life. A biblical theology of sexuality and the image of

God would prevent us from engaging in promiscuous sex or enslaving a fellow human being.

Another clear example is Titus 2:1–15. Paul urges Titus to teach "what is appropriate to sound doctrine" (Titus 2:1; see also 2:15), then specifically speaks of how the evangelist should teach (or relate to) older men, younger men, older women, younger women, and servants (2:2–10). A godly lifestyle is the goal (2:11–14). It's all about Christian character—no abstruse theology here! Thus we see conclusively that doctrine is intimately connected with lifestyle. Human morality is ultimately derived from the character and being of God. That is why understanding and studying God (which is the meaning of the word "theology") naturally leads to consideration of the way we choose to live our lives.

Doctrine Is Teaching

Again, at its basic level, doctrine is teaching. It is the substance of what we believe and think, and what we teach others. Worldviews are like opinions—everybody has one. But how biblical is our doctrine? We have found that clear thinking about what the Bible says is rarer than you might think. This is not only because there are tens of thousands of dissenting groups claiming to speak for God and assuming their interpretation of Scripture to be correct. That is confusing enough, like the ancient labyrinth that Theseus attempted to find his way out of.

The tangled hedge of human teachings also originates in a failure to think logically and consistently—let alone biblically.

As we discern in Jesus' Sermon on the Mount, to cite a familiar example, doctrine is not bare teaching, but *teaching us how to live.*

Life and Doctrine, Reconsidered

Later in 1 Timothy, Paul tells Timothy to watch his life and doctrine: "Keep a close watch on yourself and on the teaching. Persist in this, for by so doing you will save both yourself and your hearers" (1 Timothy 4:16 ESV). Is it certain that this primarily means believing the correct things? It is worthwhile to take a closer look at the passage in its context. When we read the entire paragraph, rather than an isolated verse, we soon notice what Paul means by "doctrine." 1 Timothy 4:12 refers to life (speech, conduct, love, faith, purity), while 1 Timothy 4:13 refers to doctrine (the public reading of Scripture, with preaching from these readings). Thus "doctrine" in 4:16 refers not so much to one's creed or theological convictions as it does to one's public teaching.

Of course, this teaching should honor and line up with the word of God. Yet knowledge (or theology) was never an end in itself, since the goal is to know God and share in his holiness (2 Peter 1:3–4). Life and doctrine are not two separate things, like the wings of an aircraft.

They are more like two sides of a coin.[3]

Furthermore, an excessive emphasis on doctrine, in the way many modern people think of it, is simply not in line with the thrust of Jesus' teaching. Although he was a teacher (remember, doctrine is teaching), he placed relatively little emphasis on technical theology. In fact, he constantly ran up against the teachers of the law (NIV; scribes, in the older versions), who focused on obscure technical matters of theology and interpretation, whereas Jesus focused on teaching people to live the way God wanted us to live. Or consider the parable of the Pharisee and the Tax Collector (Luke 18:9–14). It was not the learned Pharisee who received God's approval, but the humble and repentant tax collector. In Samaria the unlearned and (hitherto) immoral woman at the well (John 4) proves to be a far better teacher than Jesus' own disciples (see also Luke 7:36–50).

Sound and Unsound Doctrine

What exactly, then, is "sound doctrine"? The phrase appears in seven passages in the Pastoral Epistles (1 Timothy 1:10; 4:6; 6:3; 2 Timothy 1:13, 4:3; Titus 1:9; 2:1). It refers to lifestyle, behaviors, and attitudes, not technical theology. "Sound" is a medical word referring to being healthy and whole, with everything functioning as it should. In God's word, spiritual health is the goal—becoming mature, like Christ (Romans 8:29; 12:1–2;

Philippians 3:8–14; Colossians 1:28–2:1).

Unsound doctrines and doctrinal systems are like viruses, infecting everything and making the entire system slow and sluggish. The human teachings we will examine in this book are those that accompany and often cause spiritual disease and dysfunction.

How Sound Doctrine Is Practical

It enhances our understanding of Scripture.
It equips us to help others.
It bolsters confidence.
It improves our discernment.
It makes us gracious toward others.

The Pastoral Epistles also speak of church discipline (1 Timothy 1:20; 5:20; Titus 1:11; 3:10). Discipline, including disfellowship, was normally for *refusal to live a holy life* (1 Corinthians 5:11–13). Disfellowship was not usually for entertaining distorted unbiblical ideas—unless the teacher was deliberately leading others away from the gospel (2 Timothy 2:17). In most modern churches, however, this discipline is more likely to take place when someone entertains what the group considers wrong views on the end times, baptism, the Spirit, or eternal security, than when the person is involved in gossip, materialism, or drunkenness.

In many churches, historically speaking, greater

emphasis has been placed on fully understanding the mechanics of salvation than on following the Savior. (Often you are accepted as a member if you show up to church, take weekly communion, and support the church financially—whether or not your life shows evidence of holiness or serious intent to live as a disciple of Christ.) Persons living holy lives outside one's own fellowship tend to be viewed with suspicion; interacting with them may be regarded as dangerous. One must certainly not consider them as saved, nor may one marry them. Great emphasis has also been placed on the dangers of allowing musical instruments in worship, emotional expressions of faith, and cooperating with other congregations in any organization or hierarchy above the local church level.

Is "Doctrine" Inherently Ungracious?

Isn't insisting on biblical correctness ungracious—telling others, or implying, that they are wrong? In our current "Judge not!" climate, many no doubt think so. But doctrine is the content of what we teach, and Christianity makes some claims, things held to be true. (The Son of God came to earth in human form; there is a judgment day; we are to pursue holiness, not happiness; to name just a few.) These propositions may be false, or they may be true—one or the other. If they are false, religion is no big deal—at least not the faith Jesus taught us. But if they are true, certain obligations follow as we align ourselves with the truth. To ask Christ-followers to downplay or ignore doctrine is to ask them to downplay or ignore the Scriptures. It is also to refuse to take the claims of Jesus seriously. Quite simply, if he spoke the truth, we must take a stand.

If we care about others, we will speak the truth. This does not mean running roughshod over others, inflicting our opinions on them, or clobbering them with the "whole counsel of God" (Acts 20:27 NKJV) without allowing them time to process. Christians are to speak graciously (Colossians 4:5–6). As Christ's representatives, we declare the truth that sets us free (2 Corinthians 4:2; John 8:32). If we keep silent, it is because we don't care. Since Christianity makes claims about how to live, what is meaningful, and what happens after death, *not* to speak is ungracious. It is to deprive others of the opportunity to hear the gospel. It is withholding the good news about Jesus and what he taught.

Must Doctrine Be Technical?

Here is where things can get sticky. We want to talk about God and his word. But there are so many conflicting opinions out there, and sometimes we don't know how to explain ourselves or counter an interpretation we know runs counter to biblical teaching. This is where *Informed* can help.[4]

Yet even if we have good answers to the questions

people are asking, some folks find the very notion of doctrine distasteful. It is often associated with off-putting words like "dogma," "argument," "sectarian," "denomination," and "theology." Of course, the substance of doctrine may be technical theology: teaching on the Trinity, eschatology (last things), predestination, and so on. To converse intelligently on some matters requires a degree of biblical depth, and that may require years of maturing as a believer, along with biblical training. Yet more often than not, it's simpler than that. Many biblical doctrines are easy to grasp, and many off-base teachings are easy to refute. That is the aim of our book: to help us distinguish human teaching and tradition from biblical truth.

The Paradigm Must Change

Once again, in the Bible doctrine entails behaviors more than beliefs. And although it is a lot easier to define oneself by a list of beliefs than by a set of Christlike behaviors, viewing "doctrine" as points of theology that prove our group to be right and others wrong is not in line with biblical teaching. Obviously, this is not to say that every hymn-singing group is on track and pleasing to the Lord. There is a lot of destructive teaching out there, and we need to be sober about the risks (2 Peter 3:1–3).

However, when spiritual leaders fail to confront unchristian living (worldliness and failure to live out the gospel), instead policing the fellowship only to enforce theological conformity, we err. Worse, we fail to demonstrate Christ to the world. We are inevitably marked by division, compromise, and worldliness. If we focused more on modeling holy and Christlike lives and less on maintaining uniformity of interpretation, would we not be more unified as God's people, striving to think, speak, and act like our Savior? Wouldn't we also be more effective?

Summary

Sound Doctrine Is Not:

- *A weapon.* Jesus did not intend doctrine to be a theological construct used to evaluate, label, and demonize others, or to keep them at arm's length. It is easy to rely on prooftexts, creeds, and shibboleths (Judges 12:4–6). The Lord, however, would have us build bridges, not destroy them. True, the Word is a hammer that breaks rocks in pieces (Jeremiah 23:29), but it is the Lord who smashes. The world does not need more "Bible bangers."
- *Primarily intellectual.* It is not right to exalt understanding above obedience. While we must place a high premium on truth and diligently reject falsehood, the theological errors that are especially

dangerous are the ones that deflect us from the narrow road (Matthew 7:13–14), that is, away from holy living. "The narrow gate is not, as so often assumed, doctrinal correctness. The narrow gate is obedience—and the confidence in Jesus necessary to it... The broad gate, by contrast, is simply doing whatever I want to do."[5]

- *Technical or abstruse.* Although some sections of Scripture are difficult to navigate (2 Peter 3:15–16), the authors of the Bible never aimed for pedantry or complicated vocabulary. They wrote for the average person, and in a way that, for the most part, could be readily understood (2 Corinthians 1:13).
- *Ungracious.* There is nothing unchristian about emphasizing doctrine, provided we do so with biblical sensitivity and genuine concern for others.

Sound Doctrine Makes Us:

- *Obedient.* Sound doctrine concerns life lived in obedience to the gospel. "Life and doctrine" (1 Timothy 4:16) refers to holy living in line with the word of God. This does not mean equal emphasis on obedience and correctness—at least correctness as defined by a single religious group.
- *Spiritually healthy.* Sound (healthy) teaching brings spiritual health, as surely as unsound (unhealthy)

teaching has its own pathology: lowered resistance to sin and worldliness, increased focus on self, lack of healthful spiritual habits (poor "diet" and little "exercise"), and worse.

- *Humble.* The more we study the Word, the more we realize we don't understand. Between us we have read through the entire Bible seventy or eighty times—and this has not served to diminish our sense of awe at the depth and power of the Word. Nor has it slaked our thirst for the Scriptures. Just the opposite.
- *Confident.* Gaining familiarity with all Scripture (2 Timothy 3:16), pondering it (2 Timothy 2:7), discerning what is more important and what is less weighty (Matthew 23:23–24), and appreciating the practical application of the Bible's great themes, stories, and commands gives us confidence to share the good news. (Of course, serious students of the Word are not serious enough if they are not actively helping others.)
- *Effective.* Since God's word is powerful and effective (Isaiah 55:10–11; Hebrews 4:12–13), when the people of God are properly equipped (2 Timothy 3:15–17), their lives have a positive spiritual impact. And isn't that something we all want?

While doctrine should be (for the most part) easy to understand, religious teachers have constructed a bewildering maze of opinions and agendas. In the next chapter, we will start with the most common false construct, ***Clergy & Laity.***

2

Clergy & Laity – The Most Common (and Destructive) False Construct

This system is prevalent not only in churches, but in virtually every human organization. Of all the doctrinal systems under investigation in this book, Clergy & Laity may be the most dangerous.

When I (Douglas) was about seven years old, a monk spoke at our school, sharing about the vows he had taken, as well as about his simple lifestyle. There were two sorts of Christians, he explained. Some were wholly devoted to God, living for him "full time." Others went to church and did religious things, but were not at all expected to give everything up for the Lord. All the same, something in my soul responded, "I should live that way, too."

Not only did I admire the monk, but I was drawn to something in him: the holy. For us, that meant grand hymns, waxen candles, and uniformed clergy. It was not obvious that this entailed an unhealthy double standard. I still remember the words of a song I heard around that time:

I sing a song of the saints of God,
Patient and brave and true:
They toiled and they fought and they lived
 and they died
For their own good Lord they knew.
And one was a doctor and one was a priest
And one was slain by a fierce, wild beast;
And there's no, not a reason, no not the least,
Why I shouldn't be one too!

My conscience was mildly haunted by the words of that song for many years—especially by the thought of being slain by a beast. Could there be something so worth living for that it was also worth dying for? The words remained in my heart until I began to consider the Bible more seriously.

At age sixteen, several months after a "born-again" experience within a neighborhood charismatic fellowship, an unusual invitation came my way. The leaders asked us if anyone was interested in becoming a disciple—that is, a Christian of a higher order of commitment. They said we would meet every Thursday night in one of the men's homes. (I attended what turned out to be a few discussions of the book of Daniel, with no sustained call to Christian commitment except to show up for the lessons.) It was explicitly taught that not all Christians needed to be disciples—we would not want to "judge" those who

declined to commit. It was okay to be a spe
sort of religion wasn't especially inspiring.

Looking back now, I believe I was waiting for an opportunity—an invitation—to commit to a life of holiness. When, at university, I met men and women who lived as committed a life as the one they taught (and sang) about, the old chords were set vibrating, and I knew that my quest, in one sense, was at an end.

As for me (Joseph), I have had many experiences and encounters with different religious and spiritual groups and belief systems in my life, despite only holding firmly to two: the one in which I was raised and the one I am in now. The one in which I was raised espouses and teaches a strong and clearly defined clergy-laity structure. Even within the clergy, there are levels within levels of differing expectations for spiritual commitment. I believe that most Christian denominations, groups, and fellowships end up with some form of separating the leadership or the deeply devoted from everyone else. Jesus called his disciples from all walks of life and with drastically differing political and sometimes even religious belief systems. Yet his call to everyone was the same: "Follow me." To be fair, the fellowship I grew up in did also have high official standards for all believers, but in practice it was commonly understood and felt that the clergy in all its ranks, as well as those in religious orders, were somehow more devoted, more holy, and more spiritual than the est of us. I think that is what many, perhaps even most people, think about their own church: *"The ministers either are or should be better and more spiritual than I am."* This way of thinking, as we shall see, does a great disservice to the teachings of our Lord, to ourselves, to people new to the faith, and even to professional or paid ministers.

So, are there two levels of commitment? Are all Christians ministers, or is the typical division between doers and watchers okay with the Lord?

What This Belief Teaches

Professionals handle the work of "ministry." Terms used are clergy, laity, lay leader, minister, etc.

- *Laity* = "Body of religious worshipers, as distinguished from the clergy"
- *Clergy* = "Group or body of ordained persons in a religion, as distinguished from the laity"

Normally the clergy are paid. There are two standards of commitment; laity are not expected to have the same level of devotion as clergy.

The Actual Biblical Emphasis

Leadership is good; we should respect our leaders and those who work hard.

We all have different levels of ability, and we function in different ways. Not everyone influences others in the same way. Some have gifts of leadership, while others do not.

Some ministries and works require large investments of time normally unavailable to those with "secular" jobs, families, and other responsibilities.

Favored Biblical Texts

A few of the passages used to support this teaching are:

2 Timothy 4:1–5

> *In the presence of God and of Christ Jesus, who will judge the living and the dead, and in view of his appearing and his kingdom, I give you this charge: Preach the word… But you, keep your head in all situations, endure hardship, do the work of an evangelist, discharge all the duties of your ministry.*

Biblical error: Evangelists are always "full-time," paid church workers.

Correcting the error: An evangelist is an apostolic emissary. Evangelists planted churches and then moved on. They did not normally remain, settling into a "senior pastor" role. When there was insufficient support for evangelists (missionaries), they worked to support themselves. This also afforded ins into the towns where they were ministering.

In 2 Timothy 4, Paul does not *appoint* Timothy an evangelist; he has already been one for perhaps fifteen years. Paul merely *reminds* Timothy about the charge. This is not to say that it is necessarily wrong to formally appoint (ordain) a person to a certain ministry. The recognition and clarity an appointment brings are positive consequences. But the only leaders about whom any formal process of selection or appointment appears in the New Testament are elders and deacons (1 Timothy 3:1–13; Titus 1:5–9).

This error is reinforced by some translations. The NIV (quoted above) paraphrases 2 Timothy 4:5. It is more accurately translated "fulfill your ministry," in the ESV and the NASB, for example. Like Acts 6:4, this has a narrow and clear focus: to bring others to Christ through church planting. On the other hand, "discharge all the duties of your ministry" is like a blank check, with ministers expected to excel in preaching, teaching, counseling, planning, discipling, weddings, funerals, website maintenance and brochure design. No wonder most church members sit back and watch, instead of taking an active role! It is because the clergy are doing all the work of the ministry.

Ephesians 4:11–13

So Christ himself gave the apostles, the prophets, the evangelists, the pastors and teachers, to equip his people for works of service, so that the body of Christ may be built up until we all reach unity in the faith and in the knowledge of the Son of God and become mature, attaining to the whole measure of the fullness of Christ.

Biblical error: The clergy-laity distinction is made by Christ himself.

Correcting the error: Far from justifying a clergy-laity distinction, this passage explains that Christ gave Spirit-gifted leadership to build up the body of Christ and "to equip his people." The gifts of leadership take their place among the many gifts of the Spirit used by Christ to build up his body (see Romans 12 and 1 Corinthians 12). All Christians are spiritually gifted, and all are necessary for the proper functioning and growth of the body (1 Corinthians 12).

Hebrews 13:7, 17 ESV

Remember your leaders, those who spoke to you the word of God. Consider the outcome of their way of life, and imitate their faith... Obey your leaders and submit to them, for they are keeping watch over your souls, as those who will have to give an account. Let them do this with joy and not with groaning, for that would be of no advantage to you.

Biblical error: Leadership decisions are not to be

questioned.

Correcting the error: We are to obey church leaders, whether elders or small group leaders. Yet universal, unconditional obedience to leaders is too broad a take on these verses.

Verse 7 probably refers to an earlier generation of leaders, now dead (see also Hebrews 2:3), while verse 17 almost certainly refers to elders (probably serving as house church leaders). 1 Timothy 5:17–18 implies that at least some elders were paid for their work, though it is far from clear that this was the norm.

Exodus 18:17–23

> *Moses' father-in-law replied, "What you are doing is not good. You and these people who come to you will only wear yourselves out. The work is too heavy for you; you cannot handle it alone. Listen now to me and I will give you some advice, and may God be with you. You must be the people's representative before God and bring their disputes to him. Teach them his decrees and instructions, and show them the way they are to live and how they are to behave. But select capable men from all the people—men who fear God, trustworthy men who hate dishonest gain—and appoint them as officials over thousands, hundreds, fifties and tens. Have them serve as judges for the people at all times, but have them bring every difficult case to you; the simple cases they can decide themselves.*

> *That will make your load lighter, because they will share it with you. If you do this and God so commands, you will be able to stand the strain, and all these people will go home satisfied."*

Biblical error: This verse is used to support a top-down leadership structure. The higher up the hierarchy, the more the leader needs to be "full time," like Moses.

Correcting the error: This method of organization had a specific purpose: to lighten Moses' workload, a hierarchy of leadership was employed for conflict resolution. At most, this tells us how the Israelite tribes were structured during their period in the desert—there is no indication that such a structure was utilized afterward. And nothing in the context of the passage requires or even implies a necessary application to church employment.

New Testament Terminology (Greek and Latin)

- ***Apostolos:*** missionary. Specifically, an eyewitness of the risen Christ (Acts 1:21–22; 1 Corinthians 9:1)
- ***Prophētēs:*** prophet. Specifically, one gifted with supernatural insight into the Scriptures (Ephesians 2:20; 3:5; 4:11).
- ***Diakonos:*** servant. ***Diakonoi*** focused on meeting the needs of the poor within the Christian community (Acts 6:1–6; 1 Timothy 3:8–13; Philippians 1:1).

- *Didaskolos:* teacher. One who instructs, teaches, builds up, and edifies others. In the New Testament, specifically one who instructs and explains the word of God and teachings of Jesus to edify and build up the body of Christ (Ephesians 4:11-13; Acts 13:1; 1 Corinthians 12:28–29; James 3:1–18).
- *Evangelistēs:* a preacher of good news (2 Timothy 4:5; Ephesians 4:11; Acts 21:8). Evangelists moved around, receiving room and board for their work. It is not necessarily wrong to employ a preacher (as a vocation); social conditions were very different in the first century. While itinerant ministries do exist in more advanced societies, nowadays traveling evangelists are perhaps more common in the Two-Thirds World.
- *Presbyteros:* an older man; in the context of leadership, an elder (1 Timothy 5:17–22; Titus 1:5–9; 1 Peter 5:1–4).
- *Episkopos:* overseer (i.e., an elder) (Philippians 1:1; 1 Timothy 3:1; Titus 1:5–9).
- *Poimēn:* shepherd (i.e., an elder). Note that ***presbyteros, poimēn,*** and ***episkopos*** are used interchangeably in Acts 20:17ff and 1 Peter 5.
- *Mathētēs:* student, pupil (Acts 11:26). The English word "disciple" is a transliteration of the Latin word for student, which is ***discipulus.***
- *Minister:* the Latin word for servant (Greek ***diakonos***). Note: the New Testament was not written in Latin, although Latin translations appeared by the second century.

- *Pastor:* the Latin word for shepherd (in other words, an elder). This word, technically speaking, doesn't even appear in the Bible, unless we are reading the Latin Vulgate—where "pastor," shepherd, is a common word.)

Correcting Errors Surrounding Terminology

All Christians are ministers (servants), not just a select few. All Christians are also called to be priests. In this respect, priests are those who mediate between God and humankind, offering sacrifices and living holy lives. Note that there is no longer any official priesthood, apart from Jesus Christ's ministry as our great high priest in heaven (Hebrews 3:1; 4:14; 5:5, 10; 6:20; 8:1). It follows, then, that no special terms of address are required—no honorific titles! (Matthew 23:5–12).

There is but one leader, Jesus. That is why in the New Testament, congregations are led by elders—a plurality, avoiding the dangers of one-man rule (and autocracy).

Range

This construct is prevalent worldwide.

Impact

A clergy-laity distinction creates a culture of participants and spectators in which there are low expectations for the laity. It tends to isolate the clergy from feedback from the members, discouraging questions from the members while it creates bottlenecks as laity seek clerical approval for possible initiatives. It places a barrier between people and God.

What We Can Do

- Be willing to evaluate church traditions, whether teaching, practice, or terminology.[6]
- Reject unbiblical words, or biblical words that are used in unbiblical ways. Remind others of what the Scriptures really teach, especially those in positions of authority and influence.
- Study church history, and learn how the clergy-laity system evolved. (For example, by the mid-200s AD, Christian leaders were being called "priests.")
- Believe the Bible: All of us are in the ministry!

Conclusion

There are *not* differing standards for those called to follow Jesus. In the Great Commission of Matthew 28:16–20, Jesus commanded his followers to make followers of all people by baptizing them in the name of the Father, Son, and Holy Spirit and by teaching everyone who followed to obey *everything* that he had commanded; in so doing, they would be the beneficiaries of his promise that he would always be with those who followed him.

In the next chapter we will explore the enormously attractive gospel of ***Health & Wealth,*** *also called Prosperity Theology.*

3

Health & Wealth – The Gospel of Materialism

One of the most pervasive unsound doctrinal systems spreading among Christian believers today is the Health and Wealth gospel, also known as Prosperity Theology. We first ran into this theology in the early 1980s, although its roots are in the nineteenth century, and in the twentieth it began to build momentum after World War II.

What are the teachings of Health and Wealth? Is this completely wrongheaded, or do its proponents make some good points? Once we examine the kernel of truth in Prosperity Theology, we will examine eight of the favorite passages of this movement, and then consider its impact. We will conclude with a simple challenge for our faith.

What This Movement Teaches

God has a plan to bless us physically, spiritually, financially, relationally, medically, etc., and the degree to which we are blessed indicates our faith and spirituality. Pastors and evangelists will become rich if they are righteous, and members too have the same chance to become wealthy.

The Actual Biblical Emphasis

God is good, and he is faithful to his promises. He also cares about the whole person and does bless in all of these ways.

Favored Biblical Texts

The verses are from the ESV unless otherwise noted.

Jeremiah 29:11–14

> *"For I know the plans I have for you, declares the LORD, plans for welfare and not for evil, to give you a future and a hope. Then you will call upon me and come and pray to me, and I will hear you. You will seek me and find me, when you seek me with all your heart. I will be found by you, declares the LORD, and I will restore your fortunes and gather you from all the nations and all the places where I have driven you, declares the LORD, and I will bring you back to the place from which I sent you into exile."*

Biblical error: The passage is normally taken completely out of context in applying it to those under the new covenant.

Correcting the error: The two covenants are confused. Promises to the Jewish people under the old covenant are not all for Christians under the new covenant. We must guard against the temptation to seek interesting or encouraging groups of words—unless we understand the context and are sure our understanding is right. Verse 10, immediately before this passage, reads, "For thus says the Lord: When seventy years are completed for Babylon, I will visit you, and I will fulfill to you my promise and bring you back to this place." This refers to a period of time two generations later![7]

Deuteronomy 6:10–12

> *"And when the LORD your God brings you into the land that he swore to your fathers, to Abraham, to Isaac, and to Jacob, to give you—with great and good cities that you did not build, and houses full of all good things that you did not fill, and cisterns that you did not dig, and vineyards and olive trees that you did not plant—and when you eat and are full, then take care lest you forget the LORD, who brought you out of the land of Egypt, out of the house of slavery."*

Biblical error: The historical context, the conquest of Canaan, is completely ignored in applying this verse to Christians. Prosperity Theology discourages people from discipline and work. Instead, they put their hope in religious acts, sorcery, or giving money to the church—believing that this will make them wealthy.

Correcting the error: The passage is for the ancient Jews, not the Christians. (We do not take over others' homes and fields in anything corresponding to Old Testament Canaan.)

Matthew 6:33

"But seek first the kingdom of God and his righteousness, and all these things will be added to you."

Biblical error: Once again, the promise has been lifted out of context. Prosperity in biblical times did not mean riches and luxury. It meant having enough food to survive, a good name in the community, and children and grandchildren to carry on the family name.

Correcting the error: This promise is only *general* (not all Christians are provided for; many are poor or languishing in prison). Besides, Jesus is speaking here of food, drink, and clothing (basic level), not the luxury items of rich Western culture. He even warns repeatedly of the dangers of riches: Luke 6:24; 8:14; 16:14–15; 18:24.

Mark 11:24

Therefore I tell you, whatever you ask in prayer, believe that you have received it, and it will be yours.

Biblical error: This passage is the primary support for "word-faith" theology—which holds that we realize (make real) our dreams by "naming and claiming" them. This is a mind-over-matter view of how to get things from God, borrowed from Eastern philosophy.

Correcting the error: Jesus emphasizes our need to forgive others—otherwise our prayers will be ineffective, and our Father in heaven may not forgive us (Mark 11:25).

1 Chronicles 4:10

> *Jabez called upon the God of Israel, saying, "Oh that you would bless me and enlarge my border, and that your hand might be with me, and that you would keep me from harm so that it might not bring me pain!" And God granted what he asked.*

Biblical error: Repetition of this prayer miraculously brings about God's material blessings and protection.

Correcting the error: The original Hebrew may mean that Jabez prayed to be kept from harming others—not to be spared pain himself. The NIV may even have mistranslated the passage, affecting the understanding of evangelicals like Bruce Wilkinson, who seized upon the prayer of Jabez and wrote a major bestseller, *The Prayer of Jabez: Breaking Through to the Blessed Life.*

Making avoidance of suffering and unpleasantness such a high priority is contrary to the call to all disciples to carry their cross (Luke 9:23).

Proverbs 29:18 (KJV)

Where there is no vision, the people perish: but he that keepeth the law, happy is he.

Biblical error: This verse is often misused, claimed as a promise that our dreams will come true. This humanistic approach reinforces individualism and can even lead to narcissism.

Correcting the error: In the Bible, visions came to the prophets, and they preached the Word (Isaiah 1:1; Daniel 2:19; Obadiah 1:1; Micah 3:6; Joel 2:28–29). When Peter cites Joel 2 (Acts 2:16–17), the context is prophecy. There is nothing here about aspirations, hopes, or a me-directed plan waiting to be discovered. The older verbiage of the KJV is misleading, since in the modern West, vision is associated with self-confidence, not miraculous revelation. The ESV translates it better: "Where there is no prophetic vision the people cast off restraint, but blessed is he who keeps the law."

John 10:10

The thief comes only to steal and kill and destroy. I came that they may have life and have it abundantly.

Biblical error: This error stems from reading wrong theology into the passage. What exactly is abundant living? Luxurious living, or life as the Lord intended it to be lived?

Correcting the error: How did Jesus live the abundant life? Did any of it have to do with wealth, prestige, or material comfort? Rather, did he not renounce such things? Prosperity preachers are crooked and deceitful. They know very well that the abundant life Jesus promised *and lived* has nothing to do with riches (see 1 Corinthians 1:26–27; 4:1–11).

We were struck when rereading *The Imitation of Christ* (Thomas à Kempis). This passage is apropos:

> Many love Jesus so long as no troubles happen to them. Many praise him and bless him, so long as they receive comforts from him. But if Jesus hides himself and seems to withdraw from them for even a little while, they immediately begin complaining or feel a great sense of dejection... Shouldn't all those constantly seeking his blessing be called mercenaries?[8]

Romans 8:28

> *And we know that for those who love God all things work together for good, for those who are called according to his purpose.*

Biblical error: The Prosperity Gospel does not respect the context of this important passage. Misreading this passage easily reinforces Visions and Dreams theology (see Chapter 11). This is not following the example of Christ and his disciples!

Correcting the error: The verse that follows this one is: "For those whom he foreknew he also predestined to be conformed to the image of his Son, in order that he might be the firstborn among many brothers." The "for" indicates that verse 29 is explaining verse 28. This is not a promise that in the end we will get our dream job (or dream girl, dream house, etc.). Since the image of Jesus includes much suffering, it means that all things work together for character formation through suffering. Providence is not unalterable destiny. There isn't necessarily only one right choice when it comes to career, marriage, or residence.

Range

Extremely common among evangelicals, Health and Wealth teaching characterizes 95% or more of charismatic churches. It is normative in Africa, Latin America, much of Asia, and much of North America.

Impact

Prosperity Theology encourages an infantile focus on physical things. It also fuels materialism amd self-indulgence. This is an ultimately futile cycle: craving for status leads to overspending and debt (Proverbs 22:7).

Concluding Challenge

Don't be taken in by this shallow and unbiblical theology, or by the dishonest preachers who, by teaching it, fleece their flocks and fill them with false hopes.

Think Critically

- Read passages in context.
- Don't take the preacher's (or author's) word for it.
- Weigh every claim. Does it make sense biblically?
- Does it fit well with the big picture of biblical theology?
- Dig into the Word!

Resist Materialism

- For our modern society, there is something seductive about Health and Wealth teaching.
- Honor scriptural teaching on wealth and possessions.
- Have nothing to do with materialistic Christianity—for how is this Christian?
- Be a good steward of God's blessings and the fruits of your labor so you can give to those truly in need!

*In our next chapter we will explore the hysteria and history behind **"Signs & Wonders."***

4

Signs & Wonders – History and Hysteria

The doctrine(s) referred to in this chapter regard the specific belief that a faithful Christian today can, and in some cases *should*, perform the same type of miracles that the apostles did in the New Testament. A popular case of this doctrine is in the Pentecostal movement, where "speaking in tongues" is taught to be a sign of great faith, and even proof of a baptism by the Holy Spirit. Also in the Pentecostal movement, there are many gatherings of miraculous healings, anecdotes of unbelievable feats, and sometimes even absurd claims.

God is alive and well, and he has the right and the ability to perform miracles whenever, however, and through whomever he chooses. Even so, his miracles in the Old Testament and New Testament alike were few and far between, and each served a specific purpose at a specific time. In the same way, the apostles were given abilities to perform miracles unlike anyone has had since. The signs and wonders shown in the early church by the apostles were specifically to confirm God's word "by the signs that accompanied it" (Mark 16:20). The apostles were given a daunting task—start the Christian faith in the nations! Often, the signs and wonders shown through them were performed to add wisdom and credibility to a faith no one had ever heard of before (ever before on earth in history!).

The doctrine of Signs and Wonders as it is often understood is unsound and unbiblical. Here we will examine several scriptures and the belief systems that incorrectly claim support from them.

First, let's plainly define the system of Signs and Wonders.

What This Movement Teaches

Miracles are essential for evangelism. Jesus and the apostles worked wonders, and Jesus is the same today (Hebrews 13:8), so we can perform miracles, too. The apostolic age did not end with the passing of the apostles. Further, when someone does not receive a miracle, we can assume there is a lack of faith on their part.

The Actual Biblical Emphasis

God is all-powerful. He performs miracles. God is real, and we should expect to experience his presence and action in our lives. God is always working and can work in any way he chooses. In the Bible, God intervened in human history through the outbreaking of miraculous signs and wonders primarily at three points in history:

1. The Exodus and Conquest
2. The prophetic ministries of Elijah and Elisha
3. The ministries of Jesus and the Twelve (+ Paul)

Favored Biblical Texts

The following four passages in the Bible are commonly used out of context to create this belief system. All excerpts are from the ESV unless otherwise noted.

John 4:48

> *So Jesus said to him, "Unless you see signs and wonders you will not believe."*

Biblical error: This passage is used to claim that for people to believe or have faith in Jesus, they must first see signs and wonders performed.

Correcting the error: Let's look at the verse in context:

> *So he came again to Cana in Galilee, where he had made the water wine. And at Capernaum there was an official whose son was ill. When this man heard that Jesus had come from Judea to Galilee, he went to him and asked him to come down and heal his son, for he was at the point of death.* ***So Jesus said to him, "Unless you see signs and wonders you will not believe."*** *The official said to him, "Sir, come down before my child dies." Jesus said to*

> *him, "Go; your son will live." The man believed the word that Jesus spoke to him and went on his way. As he was going down, his servants met him and told him that his son was recovering. So he asked them the hour when he began to get better, and they said to him, "Yesterday at the seventh hour the fever left him." The father knew that was the hour when Jesus had said to him, "Your son will live." And he himself believed, and all his household. This was now the second sign that Jesus did when he had come from Judea to Galilee* (John 4:46–54).

In its full context, this verse is an expression of frustration, not the assertion of a prerequisite for faith. The man takes Jesus at his word without first being given a sign, and the son is healed based on his father's faith before he even gets back home to see the miracle that has occurred.

Mark 16:20

> *And they went out and preached everywhere, while the Lord worked with them and confirmed the message by accompanying signs.*

Biblical error: This passage is used to claim that God normatively confirms his word through miracles. In other words, one should expect to perform miracles to confirm that one is preaching God's word.

Correcting the error: Mark 16:20 simply states that God confirmed his word with miracles in the apostolic generation. Jesus' prediction that the Word would be confirmed with miracles has already been fulfilled by the apostles (for more details, see the Acts of the Apostles). There is nothing in the passage that implies that miraculous confirmation of the Word would be an ongoing state of affairs for all people of all times, and the book of Acts indicates that these signs were primarily done by the apostles of Jesus and not generally.

John 14:12

> *"Truly, truly, I say to you, whoever believes in me will also do the works that I do; and greater works than these will he do, because I am going to the Father."*

Biblical error: This passage is used to claim that since Jesus said we would do greater things than he did, we should be performing even greater signs, wonders, and miracles than he did.

Correcting the error: John 14:12 is not referring to miracles, but to ministry impact. Entire books have been written about the lasting and transformative impact of Christianity on the world, including on things such as medical care, humanitarianism, disaster relief, care for the elderly, care for orphans and widows, legal systems, various social justice movements, nonviolence, and much more. In terms of signs, wonders, and miracles, however, no one ever did greater miracles than Jesus.

Hebrews 13:8

Jesus Christ is the same yesterday and today and forever.

Biblical error: This passage is used to claim that since Jesus is the same at all times, his expectation that we would all perform signs and wonders to help people believe in him (John 4:48), to confirm his word (Mark 16:20), and to do even greater things than Jesus did has not and will never change. Signs and wonders were not limited to the time of Jesus and the apostles, but are for all times and places because Jesus is the same for all times and all places.

Correcting the error: Hebrews 13:8 refers to the person and character of Christ, not to miracles—which are extremely rare through most of biblical history. Jesus himself is the same person at all times. He is consistent and not fickle in his character. Even Jesus was not able to perform miracles at some times and in certain places (e.g., Mark 6:5–6; Matthew 13:58).

Range

The belief that miraculous signs and wonders should accompany the proclamation of the gospel in modern times is especially prevalent in the global charismatic movement, as well as in many evangelical churches.

Impact

Like children accustomed to sugary snacks and drinks, too many in the Signs and Wonders movement live for a miraculous "high." Gimmicks, thrills, and kicks do not create spiritual maturity. Sensationalism trumps common sense when one focuses on showy, visible signs and miraculous events. Ironically, an undue focus on such things often cheapens the value and lessens the impact of what God is actually doing in people's lives.

Conclusion

God still does wonders, but be wary when people make claims that they themselves (rather than God) are wonderworkers. Focus on what God is doing in people's lives according to the Scriptures. Take care not to miss the amazing transformations of character, disposition, and impact that he makes in the lives of individuals.

In the next chapter we will comment on the common obsession with predicting the end of the world.

5

Fear & Fascination – Futile Speculation

"Fear and fascination" is a term we use to refer to obsession with end-time events. Whereas Jesus and Paul discouraged speculation, this movement revels in it. I (Joseph) remember reading Hal Lindsey's *The Late, Great Planet Earth* as a teenager and believing that the author was opening up the book of Revelation to me personally. Every time I watched the news, I saw clear signs of the world's imminent demise. Several times in subsequent years I heard famous preachers on the radio predicting the exact date that the world would end. I remember wondering even then how they could do that, since Jesus said that not even he himself knew the exact day and hour he would return! (e.g., Mark 13:32ff).

Truth be told, pretty much every century since the first has seen outbreaks of end-times fascination (if not hysteria). Although no one knows for sure all of the factors that give rise to these movements, there are certain common cues: wars and rumors of wars, an outlier regional or national economic environment (either extreme prosperity or extreme poverty), turnings of centuries or especially millennia (i.e., years ending in 99, 00, 01, or 000), years with other mathematical, calendric or numerological significance, and several other factors. What are we to make of this?

What This Movement Teaches

The world will end soon. Most often this is viewed as the entire known or civilized world of whatever period is in view, but it may also be a more local or regional or population-specific ending. Keys to understanding the coming sequence of events are hidden in the mysteries of biblical prophecy (or occasionally nonbiblical, such as Mayan or Nostradamus' prophecies), and skillful Bible expositors can unlock these mysteries. Modern or contemporary political entities, figures, and events are prophesied in the Bible—especially those relating to the superpowers of the time and region (e.g., such predictions in modern times might focus on the Middle East, the United States, China, and Russia) and extreme meteorological and astronomical phenomena.

The Actual Biblical Emphasis

We *should* always be ready for the end. God does assure us of a coming intervention. One day, the curtain *will* come down on the stage of world history.

While there are many apocalyptic references and predictions in the Bible—indeed there is an entire genre of biblical apocalyptic literature—these usually do not have the purpose of letting enlightened readers know the precise time of the end of all things. Instead, the purpose is to encourage and stimulate those "with ears that hear" to live such lives that they are ready at any moment, no matter when the time arrives. Another purpose of apocalyptic literature is to encourage believers undergoing persecution that the true battle has already been won in the cosmic realm and that their current struggle is only a small, yet meaningful, part of a larger vision for a future in which their "team" has already achieved victory.

Favored Biblical Texts

Matthew 24

At the beginning of chapter 24, Jesus predicts the complete destruction of the temple. A little later, his disciples ask him privately, "When will this happen, and what will be the sign of your coming and of the end of the age?" (Matthew 24:3).

He answers as follows:

> *"Watch out that no one deceives you. For many will come in my name, claiming, 'I am the Messiah,' and will deceive many. You will hear of wars and rumors of wars, but see to it that you are not alarmed. Such things must happen, but the end is still to come. Nation will rise*

against nation, and kingdom against kingdom. There will be famines and earthquakes in various places. All these are the beginning of birth pains…

"So when you see standing in the holy place 'the abomination that causes desolation,' spoken of through the prophet Daniel—let the reader understand— then let those who are in Judea flee to the mountains…

"False messiahs and false prophets will appear and perform great signs and wonders to deceive, if possible, even the elect. See, I have told you ahead of time.

"So if anyone tells you, 'There he is, out in the wilderness,' do not go out; or, 'Here he is, in the inner rooms,' do not believe it. For as lightning that comes from the east is visible even in the west, so will be the coming of the Son of Man. Wherever there is a carcass, there the vultures will gather.

"Immediately after the distress of those days
"'the sun will be darkened,
and the moon will not give its light;
the stars will fall from the sky,
and the heavenly bodies will be shaken.'

"Then will appear the sign of the Son of Man in heaven. And then all the peoples of the earth will mourn when they see the Son of Man coming on the clouds of heaven, with power and great glory. And he will send his angels with a loud trumpet call, and they will gather his elect from the four winds, from one end of the heavens to

the other.

> *"Now learn this lesson from the fig tree: As soon as its twigs get tender and its leaves come out, you know that summer is near. Even so, when you see all these things, you know that it is near, right at the door. Truly I tell you, this generation will certainly not pass away until all these things have happened. Heaven and earth will pass away, but my words will never pass away"* (Matthew 24:4–8, 15–16, 24–35).

Biblical error: Many individuals and groups over the years have looked to the details of Jesus' reply in this passage to discern the specific times, places, and events that will lead to "the end of the age," which is thought to occur sometime in their immediate or not very distant future. This is despite Jesus ending this private teaching session by stating repeatedly and in various ways (Matthew 24:36–51) that his disciples should:

> *"… keep watch, because* ***you do not know on what day your Lord will come.*** *But understand this: If the owner of the house had known at what time of night the thief was coming, he would have kept watch and would not have let his house be broken into. So you also must be ready, because* ***the Son of Man will come at an hour when you do not expect him"*** *(Matthew 24:42–44, emphasis added).*

In other words, he emphasizes that no one knows the precise time that these events will happen; nevertheless, he does give them some clues so that they might recognize it as it is happening.

Correcting the error: Matthew 24 refers (in historical context) to the destruction of Jerusalem (AD 70), an event that took place in the lives of many of Jesus' listeners (Matthew 24:34).[9] 1 Thessalonians 5:1–2 (which may refer to Matthew 24:36–51) indicates that we will *not* know when the end is nigh.

The last days began long ago, with the ministry of Jesus. This period lasts until the Judgment. In other words, the last days are more than the final years of earthly history; they are the overlap of the age to come with the present age—starting at Pentecost, as Peter preached (Acts 2:14–41; notice that Peter applies Joel's prophecy about the last days to the events currently occurring on the Day of Pentecost as he was speaking).

This movement also commits a meteorological error. Earthquakes, fires, floods, etc. are certainly apt images of judgment (and human powerlessness), but they do not point to the end times, as such occurrences are common in every decade of history. In other words, even if all these meteorological events happen to occur during the end times, the mere presence of such events cannot prove that any given occurrence is a definitive sign that "this must be it!"

Range

This set of beliefs is prevalent in many fundamentalist churches and fringe groups as well as in pockets within larger, more mainstream church groups. In modern times, such groups and beliefs have been appearing in various stripes since 1844 (the Millerites—followers of William Miller, who birthed the Adventist movement). In addition, there is an entire modern genre of apocalyptic- and postapocalyptic-themed novels (such as the *Left Behind* series) and films that has further popularized such ideas and firmly fixed them as part of the modern cultural mindset.

Impact

An undue focus on the end times can be a distraction from holy living. Excessive emphasis on just a few portions of Scripture leads to a lack of knowledge of the big picture of the Bible. Fear and Fascination teaching often brings discredit to the gospel message (silliness, naivety, poor stewardship of possessions—e.g., when misguidedly thrown away in the belief that they will no longer be needed). A string of failed predictions always trails behind this movement. (One day, of course, they will hit it right—by luck, not through careful biblical interpretation.)

Conclusion

How can anyone state the conclusion better than Jesus did in Matthew 6:33–34 (NLT): *"Seek the Kingdom of God above all else, and live righteously, and he will give you everything you need. So don't worry about tomorrow, for tomorrow will bring its own worries. Today's trouble is enough for today."*

Next we zero in on two popular doctrines connected with the end times: ***Rapture & Tribulation.***

6

Rapture & Tribulation – Exiting Earth?

This chapter overlaps and dovetails with the previous chapter, "Fear & Fascination" (obsession with the end times). The rather artificial scenario—that true believers will be snatched up to heaven, from which vantage point they may observe the horrors being unleashed upon unbelievers on the earth below—has become extremely popular, especially in the last 100 years. Beginning in the 1970s and continuing ever since, there has been a series of popular books, novels, and films featuring this idea or a close variant.

What This Movement Teaches

In the most common version of this doctrine, when the Lord returns, God will "rapture" the church up to heaven. Christians are thus protected from the "tribulation" (described in Revelation) that torments the damned.

The Actual Biblical Emphasis

Jesus will one day be united with his Bride, the

church (Ephesians 5:25–32), and God and the Lamb will make their home once again with a redeemed humanity (Revelation 21–22).

Etymology: "Rapture" comes from the Latin *rapire,* translating the Greek *harpadzomai* (snatch) in 1 Thessalonians 4:17. "Tribulation" derives from the Latin *tribulatio,* translating the Greek *thlipsis* (oppression, affliction). "Tribulation" is a common word in the King James Version. It most often refers to times of suffering and oppression as testing and refining for God's people, with an eventual vindication, overcoming, and victory for them.

Favored Biblical Texts

1 Thessalonians 4:16–17

> *For the Lord himself will come down from heaven, with a loud command, with the voice of the archangel and with the trumpet call of God, and the dead in Christ will rise first. After that, we who are still alive and are left will be caught up together with them in the clouds to meet the Lord in the air. And so we will be with the Lord forever.*

Biblical error: This passage is used to teach that believers will be raptured, or snatched up to heaven, so that the terrible events described in Revelation will only come upon unbelievers.

Correcting the error: While this passage does describe believers being snatched up to meet Jesus in the air, there is nothing said here that links any of this to the events described in the book of Revelation.

Biblical scholars are divided on whether meeting the Lord in the air (1 Thessalonians 4:17) is an event on the way to heaven, or a welcoming of the Lord to the earth (in which all will be made new, Revelation 21).

John 14:1–4

> *"Do not let your hearts be troubled. You believe in God; believe also in me. My Father's house has many rooms; if that were not so, would I have told you that I am going there to prepare a place for you? And if I go and prepare a place for you, I will come back and take you to be with me that you also may be where I am. You know the way to the place where I am going."*

Biblical error: This is used as support for the rapture.

Correcting the error: In context, Jesus is merely saying that he is going to his Father to prepare a place for his followers. He promises to return and take them with him but, again, makes no reference to them observing any tribulations of unbelievers. All Christians look forward to the Second Coming of the Lord and to being united with him for eternity. The promise of heaven (whether we go there or God comes to earth or there is a united New

Heaven and New Earth) takes place after the Judgment; the saved are not currently in heaven, as John 3:13 says, "No one has ever gone into heaven except the one who came from heaven—the Son of Man."

Revelation 7:9, 13–17

After this I looked, and there before me was a great multitude that no one could count, from every nation, tribe, people and language, standing before the throne and before the Lamb. They were wearing white robes and were holding palm branches in their hands…

Then one of the elders asked me, "These in white robes—who are they, and where did they come from?"

I answered, "Sir, you know."

And he said, "These are they who have come out of the great tribulation; they have washed their robes and made them white in the blood of the Lamb. Therefore,

"they are before the throne of God
and serve him day and night in his temple;
and he who sits on the throne
will shelter them with his presence.
'Never again will they hunger;
never again will they thirst.
The sun will not beat down on them,'
nor any scorching heat.
For the Lamb at the center of the throne
will be their shepherd;

'he will lead them to springs of living water.'
'And God will wipe away every tear from their eyes.'"

Biblical error: Although the descriptions of the judgments of Revelation are not literal, a doctrine of "the tribulation" is crafted from its images.

Correcting the error: In Scripture, tribulation more commonly refers to hardships faced by God's people in this life—*not* by outsiders. Notice that those dressed in white as described in this passage are the believers "who have come out of the great tribulation"! (v.14). In other words, the true believers were not snatched away to watch the events of Revelation unfold upon the unbelievers, but believer and unbeliever alike go through the great tribulation resulting from the first six seals being opened. The text does not make clear whether those who have "come out of the great tribulation" and who now stand before the throne of God have already died or been rescued or how they have come to stand before the throne.

Range

Especially prevalent in fundamentalist and evangelical churches, this doctrine was greatly accelerated through Hal Lindsey's *The Late Great Planet Earth* and Tim LaHaye's *Left Behind* series, as well as many subsequent books, movies, and novels. Some churches make this doctrine and similar end-time prophecies the central focus of their public preaching and teaching. There are also several popular radio programs that feature such teaching and preaching as a basic assumption.

Impact

As with the Fear and Fascination movement outlined in the previous chapter, focusing on rapture and tribulation can be a distraction from the mission. For some it may lead to a disregard for the earth and ecology and a lack of concern for the environment ("It's all gonna burn, baby!"). Historically and currently, there is often widespread bickering over the timing of the rapture with respect to the tribulation—even though these two events are not explicitly or implicitly linked together in the biblical text.

Conclusion

The Scriptures counsel us to think about the end of the world with sobriety and in a state of maximum readiness.

> *Now, brothers and sisters, about times and dates we do not need to write to you, for you know very well that the day of the Lord will come like a thief in the night. While people are saying, "Peace and safety," destruction will come on them suddenly, as labor pains on a pregnant*

> *woman, and they will not escape.*
>
> *But you, brothers and sisters, are not in darkness so that this day should surprise you like a thief. You are all children of the light and children of the day. We do not belong to the night or to the darkness. So then, let us not be like others, who are asleep, but let us be awake and sober. For those who sleep, sleep at night, and those who get drunk, get drunk at night. But since we belong to the day, let us be sober, putting on faith and love as a breastplate, and the hope of salvation as a helmet. For God did not appoint us to suffer wrath but to receive salvation through our Lord Jesus Christ. He died for us so that, whether we are awake or asleep, we may live together with him. Therefore encourage one another and build each other up, just as in fact you are doing* (1 Thessalonians 5:1–11).

Whereas the doctrines of eschatology (the end of the world) appeal to the emotions, the next set of teachings appeal more to the mind. They are the doctrinal legacy of Calvin.

7

Predestination & Perseverance – God's Good Pleasure?

John Calvin (1509–1564) was one of the leading thinkers of the Protestant Reformation. He retaught many of the ideas of the influential church leader Augustine, bishop of Hippo (North Africa, AD 354–430). Calvinism, the theological system fully developed and evolved from Calvin's theology by his followers after his death, is a unified and internally consistent system of interpretations, that is increasingly popular among Bible believers. Yet, despite its coherence, it does not fit well with the Scriptures, and more important, it was certainly not the teaching of the early church.

What This Belief Teaches

Among other things, this belief system teaches that God has predetermined (before anyone existed) who will be saved and lost eternally. Those whom he has chosen will persevere to the end, therefore it is impossible for them to lose their salvation.

TULIP

The modern encapsulation of Calvinist doctrine is often summarized by the acronym TULIP.

- **T**otal depravity. Since the Fall, all human beings are born without the capacity to do good on their own.
- **U**nconditional election. God has sovereignly chosen those who will be saved and lost without any reference to anything they do. Their fate is solely determined by God.
- **L**imited atonement. Jesus did not die for everyone; his death only atones for the sins of the elect (i.e., those God has already chosen for salvation).
- **I**rresistible grace. God's free and gracious gift of salvation for the elect cannot ultimately be rejected by those whom God has chosen.
- **P**erseverance of the saints. Only the elect persevere to the end; these cannot possibly lose their salvation. If someone does appear to lose their salvation, it is taken as proof that they never were among the elect in the first place.

The Actual Biblical Emphasis

Humanity in its current state is sinful. God is truly

sovereign and in control. The crucifixion succeeded in providing a way for sinful humanity to be redeemed from the effects and consequences of sin. The power of the Holy Spirit can transform sinful human beings into the likeness of Christ. We can be secure in the promises and power of God to save. From the beginning, God has made human beings in his image as co-rulers over his Creation (Genesis 1) and allows us to participate in the mystery of our salvation (Philippians 2:12–13).

Favored Biblical Texts

Many texts are used to support various Calvinistic tenets, beliefs, and principles, among them Ephesians 2:1–10, Acts 13:48; Matthew 26:28; John 6:44, and John 10:28. We are unable to do an exhaustive review of the texts used to support Calvinistic beliefs. We will look at just one of them here:

Ephesians 2:1–10

> *As for you, you were dead in your transgressions and sins, in which you used to live when you followed the ways of this world and of the ruler of the kingdom of the air, the spirit who is now at work in those who are disobedient. All of us also lived among them at one time, gratifying the cravings of our flesh and following its desires and thoughts. Like the rest, we were by nature deserving of wrath. But because of his great love for us,*

> *God, who is rich in mercy, made us alive with Christ even when we were dead in transgressions—it is by grace you have been saved. And God raised us up with Christ and seated us with him in the heavenly realms in Christ Jesus, in order that in the coming ages he might show the incomparable riches of his grace, expressed in his kindness to us in Christ Jesus. For it is by grace you have been saved, through faith—and this is not from yourselves, it is the gift of God—not by works, so that no one can boast. For we are God's handiwork, created in Christ Jesus to do good works, which God prepared in advance for us to do.*

Biblical errors: This passage (and other, similar passages) is used to support the idea that without God's grace and election, we are completely unable to do anything good because of the effects of original sin. We are in a state of total depravity from which we cannot rescue ourselves. There is absolutely nothing we can do. Only God can do something.

Correcting the errors: This sounds true because it is in part true. It is correct to say that we are unable to save ourselves and require an intervention from God in the form of Jesus Christ. However, the passage in context does not teach total depravity.

The denial of free will is contrary to both Scripture and experience; this is a philosophical question as well as a theological one, and both sides have been argued for millennia. Denying the existence of free will negates the entire doctrine of salvation "through faith," since faith requires free will in order to truly be faith.

The individual components of the philosophical system of Calvinism are refuted by hundreds of verses in the Bible (e.g., Deuteronomy 30:19, John 3:16ff, 2 Peter 3:9, Revelation 22:17, and the entire book of Hebrews!).

Some of the teachings of Calvinism may be partially true; however, they are often overemphasized or misapplied in ways that cause them not to be true as commonly understood. The doctrine of predestination, for example, is true corporately but does not necessarily apply in the same way to individuals. Also, many confuse and confound the concepts of foreknowledge and predestination. Just because God knows the future does not mean that he is personally controlling and deciding each and every thing that happens. Because God allows some things to happen, such things can be said to be "his will," but that is very different from God personally making or causing something to occur. Further, "predestination" at the individual level concerns not the events of our lives so much as the quality of our heart, that is, our conformity to the character of Christ (Romans 8:29).

Range

Calvinism has had a huge and still growing impact on Christendom and the world. Many (but not all) Baptists are Calvinistic or predestinarian. It is the doctrine of Presbyterians, Reformed, many Anglicans, and the original Churches of Christ (1660–1830). Calvin himself emphasized and exemplified the importance of a sound teaching ministry, and Calvinists have excelled at producing schools, teachers, authors, and great communicators of both God's word and the tenets of Calvinism. These teachers, new and old, continue to influence generations of believers. Some of this teaching is very good and healthy, but often some of the tenets of Calvinism are also taught in the form of assumptions without much critical review. The doctrines of Predestination and Perseverance in particular are often assumed by many non-Calvinists who may reject the rest of the system.

Impact

Though there are those who seek to minimize some of the necessary conclusions, a strong belief in so-called "hyper-Calvinism" implies that God is unjust, since he rewards and condemns people based on nothing they have done (Scripture teaches just the opposite; see for example Hebrews). Often, there may be little incentive for evangelism (though in fairness, many Calvinists have been and continue to be very evangelistic, explaining that God knows the elect, but we don't, and that God may be using us as his instruments to bring the elect to salvation).

The doctrine of perseverance is often understood and overly simplified as "Once Saved, Always Saved," which can lead to lukewarm commitment. Rather than perseverance being understood as lifelong commitment (as Calvin understood it), some believe that once they are saved there is no way they can lose their salvation and that their behavior no longer matters. This is as unscriptural as it is untrue. The system has an unbalanced understanding of divine initiative and human response, leaning so far toward the divine sovereignty end of the scale that it negates the value of our human response to God. The biblical truth is that both are important. This balance is beautifully and succinctly expressed in Paul's letter to the Philippians when he writes, "My beloved, as you have always obeyed, so now, not only as in my presence but much more in my absence, work out your own salvation with fear and trembling, for it is God who works in you, both to will and to work for his good pleasure" (Philippians 2:12–13 ESV).

Conclusion

God is truly sovereign. He created us in his image and gave us free will. Even if (as some believe) that free will was "broken" by the Fall, our brokenness is reversed in Christ. We become new in him, and he undoes the damage done by sin. God has predestined that all who follow his Son and persevere in doing so will be saved (Romans 5–8).

Next we will critique the modern opinions about sex, often justified by misguided appeals to Scripture.

8

Sex & Pleasure – The Pursuit of Happiness

The sexual revolution of the '60s and '70s has had a major impact on our world—as well as on the church of Christ. Yet we should not imagine that the origins of this revolution lie only half a century in the past. By the late nineteenth century, a growing spirit of hedonism and humanism was already changing society in shocking ways. However, the Sex and Pleasure movement, with supporting theology gladly provided by liberal theologians, has certainly gained ground quickly in the last half century.

Yet it is also true that the pursuit of pleasure, entertainment, distraction, and self-gratification has been part of the human condition from the time of the Fall. We often think of only certain categories in connection with this, but we can be pulled into this type of lifestyle and thinking by all sorts of things. For example, there was a time when I (Joseph) became addicted to a computer game that was sort of like the board game Risk. I used to stay up all night playing and go to work sleep deprived. Instead of spending time with my wife, I played a game.

It wasn't even a modern fully immersive video game or a smartphone app designed expressly to addict players. Nevertheless, the hits of dopamine caused by the short-term rewards in the game stimulated my pleasure centers and my brain's sense of reward so much that I couldn't stop. After a few conversations with my wife, I stopped playing abruptly and never played again. Though most people think of sexual things, the pursuit of pleasure can also be things like playing games, shopping (including always having the latest gadget), gossip, excessive television watching, and many other activities. Please keep that in mind as we discuss hedonism.

What This Movement Teaches

I have the right to seek pleasure and happiness in any way I see fit, provided I don't hurt others. God affirms my individuality. Everyone is special and entitled to believe and do whatever they want to. This is hedonism (from the Greek *hēdonē,* pleasure), "the pursuit of pleasure; sensual self-indulgence."

The Actual Biblical Emphasis

God is the creator of sexuality, and there is nothing shameful about it within the context that he intended. The Lord *does* care about my ultimate happiness. True, God's people should be wholeheartedly involved in a pursuit—not the pursuit of happiness, but of holiness!

Paul was right: "She who is self-indulgent is dead even while she lives" (1 Timothy 5:6 HCSB).

Favored Biblical Texts

1 John 4:7

"Dear friends, let us love one another, for love comes from God. Everyone who loves has been born of God and knows God."

Biblical error: For the Sex and Pleasure movement, "God is love" means that we may express "love" any way we wish. For many holding such beliefs, it is unloving to expect discipline.

Correcting the error: God often expresses his love for his people through discipline (Deuteronomy 8:5; Hebrews 12; Revelation 3:19). In this passage, "love" does not refer to sexual love. Sexual love has the legitimate biblical context of marriage (Hebrews 13:4; Ephesians 5:21–33).

2 Samuel 1:26

"I grieve for you, Jonathan my brother;
you were very dear to me.
Your love for me was wonderful,
more wonderful than that of women."

Biblical error: This verse is often cited and interpreted

to imply male homosexual intimacy between David and Jonathan. This was not the case.

Correcting the error: In David's time and culture, women did not associate socially with men as friends and peers. A man's closest friends and confidants would naturally be other men, especially true among soldiers and warriors, as it is even today. Civil unions and legal same-sex marriages are not biblical marriages. Marriage in the Bible is always understood as being the traditional union between two people of opposite gender. While there is no biblical barrier to people with homosexual attractions becoming Christians, active homosexual behavior is consistently prohibited in both the Old and New Testaments (e.g., 1 Corinthians 6:9–11—note that this is referring to Christians). We must keep in mind, however, that other sexual sins, such as fornication (sexual activity while unmarried) and adultery (sex with someone to whom you are not married) are mentioned far more frequently than homosexuality, and that people of all sexual orientations may be guilty of either or both of these sins. Keeping this in mind should provide some balance and restraint in any discussion of sexual behavior.

Matthew 7:1

"Do not judge, or you too will be judged."

Biblical error: This verse is frequently cited with the

implication that people who disagree are supposed to keep things general, and not be personal or specific in their critiques of views and behavior.

Correcting the error: If this is what Jesus meant, he would hardly have been able to preach the Sermon on the Mount in which this verse is contained! Christians must treat all people with love and without condemnation. This does not imply, however, that we must make no attempt at correction. Right after Jesus' admonition not to judge and not to be a hypocrite (Matthew 7:1–4), he teaches that after we have examined ourselves and removed any sinful "planks" in our own lives, we "will see clearly to remove the speck" from someone else's eye!

Range

The range of influence of this movement varies with the variety of hedonism.

- *Failure to honor marital vows:* Widespread, though especially common in liberal churches and secular society.
- *Confusion about biblical marriage and family:* Everywhere, though especially among the younger generation. Many people of all ages now consider marriage as being "optional" and consider being sexually active before marriage (which is sinful according to the Bible) to be normal and healthy. Some even believe

that they *ought* to engage in premarital sexual activity to "try out" prospective marital partners or to make sure that they are sexually experienced in order to better please their future spouse.

- *Pornography:* Ubiquitous. This is a very serious issue affecting people (including Christians) throughout the world, made even more prevalent with the rise of widespread, relatively inexpensive, and always available internet access with the illusory perception of privacy and anonymity. Regular use of pornography (especially the very graphic and extremely perverse and often violent pornography easily available to many today with the click of a mouse) can be very damaging psychologically, especially in young people.
- *Hedonism and selfishness:* Global. It encompasses an emphasis on pleasure, fun, entertainment, stimulation, sex, comfort, and leisure—as well as a sometimes skewed and overly individualized emphasis on rights, entitlements, "equality," "freedom," and personal autonomy.

Impact

Emphasis on pleasure-seeking has radically altered human culture. Yale theologian Miroslav Volf states that "ours is a culture of managed pursuit of pleasure, not a culture of sustained endeavor to lead the good life."[10]

Furthermore, unbridled lust for sexual pleasure has led to marital infidelity, the objectification of women (and men) in an epidemic of pornography, the disintegration of the nuclear family, loss of conviction in the pulpit, and loss of wholesome evangelistic confidence. The self-centeredness engendered by hedonistic culture not only erodes the traditional institutions and the very fabric of societies and cultures, it also leads to individuals who may not be able to fully grasp basic concepts such as taking personal responsibility for one's actions, altruism, deferred gratification, perseverance, and self-sacrifice. This is not an issue that only affects certain generations. The negative effects of an undue focus on personal gratification and pleasure affects people of all generations and all cultures.

Conclusion

Everything that God created is good (Genesis 1). For anything to be truly good, it must take others into account and must also have boundaries, requiring self-discipline. Learning to be happy within the contexts that God created is true happiness. May we all learn the secret of the Apostle Paul who wrote, "I have learned in whatever situation I am to be content. I know how to be brought low, and I know how to abound. In any and every circumstance, I have learned the secret of facing plenty and hunger, abundance and need. I can do all things through him who strengthens me" (Philippians 4:11b–13 ESV).

In our next chapter we train our sights on popular teachings about ***Heaven & Hell.***

9

Heaven & Hell – Instant Rewards?

Given the internet's power in spreading images of heaven and hell, it should not be surprising that sometimes these images are distorted in order to affect behavioral change. Frequently we read of people already said to be in heaven or hell. Is this biblical? (No.) Or emotions are manipulated through systems of promises and threats. Was this the apostolic way? (No.) This is not really a movement in the strict sense, but more like a set of generally held beliefs.

Background

The ancient concept of life after death pictured in the Bible was shared by many cultures, including that of the ancient Hebrews, and the same views prevailed in the later popular concepts of the afterlife common to the Greco-Roman cultures.

Ancient Concepts of the Universe and the Afterlife–A Simplified View

The ancients believed that the world consisted of the

earth, which was surrounded by several "heavens" (often depicted as between three and seven in number). The first "heaven" was the sky. In both Hebrew and Greek, as well as in many modern languages, the word for sky is the same word for heaven(s). Modern English still speaks of the sky as "the heavens" in poetry and figurative speech. Above the sky there was an invisible "firmament" or hard substance, which divided the sky from the heaven(s) above it. In modern terms we might think of the various layers of the atmosphere, eventually moving into what we call outer space. The ancients conceived of the second heavenly layer as being water (which gave the sky its blue color), and above that was another firmament in which the stars and planets were fixed. Above that (in a third or even higher "heaven") was the realm of the gods (or God).

The realm of the dead was conceived of as an underworld deep below the surface of the earth. In Hebrew this underworld was known as Sheol, and in Greek the underworld was called Hades. While there is not enough space to go into detail here, what we call hell is not really the same as Hades. Sheol/Hades is simply the place where all people go when they die; it is the realm of the dead. There is scholarly debate over whether the dead are fully conscious and aware before Judgment.

While Sheol was not a fully developed concept in Hebrew literature, by the time of Jesus, the equivalent

Hades was conceived of as having areas for different groups and purposes in the afterlife. Tartarus was an area of the underworld where powerful spiritual beings were imprisoned. Gehenna was an area where the wicked were punished, and paradise (from the Greek for "garden") was an area for the righteous dead. Not all Jews of Jesus' day believed in the resurrection of the dead. The Pharisees and followers of Jesus believed in a bodily resurrection of the dead before a final judgment; however, the Sadducees did not believe the dead are raised.

What This Belief Teaches

Immediately after death, all humans go to heaven or hell. "God sends no one to hell; we send ourselves there." Furthermore, most Christians believe that hell is unremitting and eternal punishment (nonstop, infinite torture).

The Actual Biblical Emphasis

How we live this life determines what happens in the afterlife. Heaven & hell are (or will be) realities.

Favored Biblical Texts

Hebrews 12:1; Luke 16:19–31; Mark 9:48. In addition to scriptures, anecdotal evidence is also used to support this view, in which there are many biblical errors.

Correcting the errors

- Hebrews 12 is a sports analogy, not a doctrinal comment on the afterlife maintaining that dead people are watching us.
- Luke 16:19–31 is widely understood to be a parable—and even if it were not, it describes *Hades*/being with Abraham (paradise), not heaven or hell. No one (except Jesus) is in heaven yet (John 3:13; Acts 2:34).
- Mark 9:48 does not state that humans will be kept eternally conscious. The only undying creatures in this image, based on Isaiah 66:24, are the worms.
- Immortality is conditional on obedience; the human soul is not inherently immortal (1 Timothy 6:16).
- Punishment is proportional, not infinite (Luke 12:47–48).
- In 2 Thessalonians 1, hell is privation (separation from the good that God had intended for us in heaven), punishment (God inflicts it), and perdition.
- Finally, the apostles urged people to save themselves from the corruption of sin, more than frightening or threatening them with the prospect of hell. See Acts 2:40, the various speeches and interactions in Acts, and the overall emphasis of the epistles.

Range

These longstanding misconceptions about the afterlife are nearly global.

Impact

These beliefs neglect the biblical doctrines of the resurrection of the dead and the last judgment. Many of the popular beliefs about life after death leave one susceptible to sentimental and highly subjective notions of God and the afterlife—as in Todd Burpo's *Heaven Is for Real*. It is common to hear inaccurate statements about the location of the deceased in sermons and at funerals, for example.

Conclusion

Careful reading of the book of Acts and Paul's letters shows that the apostolic preaching prominently featured the proclamation of the resurrection of the dead and a final judgment of all people. The hope of bodily resurrection was an essential feature of early Christianity: *"For if the dead are not raised, not even Christ has been raised. And if Christ has not been raised, your faith is futile and you are still in your sins. Then those also who have fallen asleep in Christ have perished. If in Christ we have hope in this life only, we are of all people most to be pitied."* (1 Corinthians 15:16–19 ESV). We believe in the resurrection of the dead and that God will judge the living and the dead and the righteous will have everlasting life.

Having discussed what the Bible says about the rewards and punishments of the afterlife, we return to the earth and the common evangelical teaching about the State of Israel.

10

Zion & Palestine – Israel and the Church

What is Zionism? Why do conservative Christians typically "support Israel"? And why does the US government pump several *billion* dollars annually into the State of Israel? Israel is the recipient of the largest amount of American foreign aid. The primary reason that the US government spends so much money on supporting the State of Israel is because of its strategic location and its similarly constructed democratic government. The reason that many religious Americans support the State of Israel is because of the view that God has established the modern nation of Israel and that modern Israel is the fulfillment of prophecy and will play a central role in still-to-be-fulfilled biblical prophecy.

The Palestinian territories, consisting of the West Bank and the Gaza Strip, are semiautonomous—like a country within a country, separated from Israeli territory by walls, fences, checkpoints, and guns. In many sad and unfortunate ways, the Palestinians are stateless. Being pro-Israel typically means being anti-Palestinian and vice versa. A friend of ours, a university professor and peace activist, explains, "If you're pro-Israel or pro-Palestine, you aren't pro-peace." (Think about it.) Then why do so many Christians support Israel?

What This Belief Teaches

Central to Yahweh's plans that culminate in the heavenly Zion are political conditions in an earthly Zion. Israel is still in a covenant relationship with God. Jesus' return is in some way connected with the conversion of all national Israel. All Christians should support the State of Israel militarily. The Palestinians are not the chosen people of God, but the enemy of America and Israel.

The Actual Biblical Emphasis

God is sovereign over history and over all nations.

Favored Biblical Texts

Joshua 21:43–45

> *So the LORD gave Israel all the land he had sworn to give their ancestors, and they took possession of it and settled there. The LORD gave them rest on every side, just as he had sworn to their ancestors. Not one of their enemies withstood them; the LORD gave all their enemies into their hands. Not one of all the LORD's good promises to Israel failed; every one was fulfilled.*

Zephaniah 3:20

"At that time I will gather you;
at that time I will bring you home.
I will give you honor and praise
among all the peoples of the earth
when I restore your fortunes
before your very eyes,"
says the LORD.

Biblical error: Passages such as these are used in support of the view that Israel is always meant to be a physical nation-state belonging to God. They (and many other similar passages) are viewed as prophecies referring to the modern State of Israel.

Correcting the error: When the modern State of Israel was created in 1948, many Palestinians (most were Christian or Muslim) were evicted from their homes, their land expropriated by the fledgling government. These actions did not fulfill prophecy. God *did* promise the land to Israel—which she received over 3000 years ago (Joshua 21:43). God also promised to bring her back from exile, in the event that she *repented* (Deuteronomy 30:1–4; see also Zephaniah 3). The Jews came back to their land in the sixth century BC, under the Persian king Cyrus (2 Chronicles 36:22–23), *not* in the years leading up to 1948. No national promise remains to be fulfilled. See also Matthew 3:7–11; 21:33–46.

The architects of modern Israel were mainly atheists and agnostics. The formation of the modern State of Israel was not accompanied by faith and repentance; it was a human undertaking. That is why many of the rabbis of Orthodox Judaism oppose Zionism for its atheism and humanism.

Range

This movement is prevalent in evangelical churches. Often the political and religious rationales for supporting Israel are mixed together and confused for one another.

Impact

On Christians: theological and financial distraction from the mission of the church. A wrongly theocratic view of both the modern nation of Israel and the United States as being biblically established and sanctioned nations, with the further implication that the policies and decisions that these two nations make—especially in Israel and including the treatment of Palestinians in Israel—is also somehow sanctioned or ordained by God.

On Palestinians: massive population displacement, expropriation of property, death, and despair.

On the Muslim world: deep distrust of the West and its religion, unfortunately construed as authentic Christianity.

Conclusion

The true Israel is not the modern nation of Israel, but rather the combined Jewish and Gentile people of God (see Romans 11 and Ephesians 2). God loves all people in all nations. He "wants all people to be saved and to come to the knowledge of the truth" (1 Timothy 2:4).

Few doctrines are more attractive than Health & Wealth (Chapter 3), but ***Visions & Dreams,*** *with its appeal to self, comes close.*

11

Visions & Dreams – It's All About Me

When I (Joseph) was a young disciple, I had great dreams and believed strongly that God had a vision for my life that involved very specific things such as who I was to marry, "full-time" ministry, and even which country I would live in as a missionary. I was very concerned that my vision would line up with God's and that I was not somehow thwarting his plans for me. What I didn't realize back then is that not even once in the Bible is "vision" or "dream" used in this modern, individualistic sense of having a dream for one's life. This has implications for fellowship, worship, evangelism, and discipleship. If we have been promoting such an individualistic message (which derives more from American business culture than from the Bible), we need to stop now—and better appreciate the *corporate* dimensions of church and Christian living.

What This Belief Teaches

Since God has a personal plan for our lives, which includes mission, marriage, residence, and career, we need to have or get a vision for this plan. Every Christian needs to have a specific vision/dream for their life.

The Actual Biblical Emphasis

When we draw close to God, we sense his presence and feel inspired and hopeful about the future. Similarly, when we are immersing ourselves in his word, we make wiser decisions. It is healthy to envision a better future—a spiritual and God-directed one. The Bible speaks of trust and hope in God as the secret of contentment (Philippians 4:12–13).

Favored Biblical Texts

Proverbs 29:18 ESV

Where there is no prophetic vision the people cast off restraint, but blessed is he who keeps the law.

Biblical error: Many modern readers assume that the vision to which the verse refers is a personal vision for oneself, as in the modern, Western business use of "vision" to refer to a long-term overall plan.

Correcting the error: As we stated in Chapter 3, the visions came to the prophets, and they preached the Word (Isaiah 1:1; Daniel 2:19; Obadiah 1:1; Micah 3:6; Joel 2:28–29), but often the people didn't heed their warnings. Some translations have something like, "Without vision" instead of "Where there is no prophetic vision." The proverb is talking about what happens when people live without God's guidance through the prophetic word in contrast to those who obey God's instruction.

Acts 2:17

"In the last days, God says,
I will pour out my Spirit on all people.
Your sons and daughters will prophesy,
your young men will see visions,
your old men will dream dreams."

Biblical error: This verse is taken totally out of context to refer to a person's dreams for their life.

Correcting the error: When Peter cites Joel (Acts 2:16), the context is prophecy. As we pointed out in Chapter 3, there is nothing here about aspirations, hopes, or an individualized plan for each of us just waiting for us to discover it. Again, as in Proverbs, the visions being spoken of here are prophetic visions. The point that God is making to Joel is that the prophetic gift will be more widely distributed among the people in the last days than it apparently was during Joel's time. In Acts 2, Peter sees the outpouring of the Holy Spirit as a fulfillment of this prophecy of Joel's (or perhaps the beginning of an ongoing fulfillment).

Jeremiah 29:11–14

> *"For I know the plans I have for you, declares the LORD, plans for welfare and not for evil, to give you a future and a hope. Then you will call upon me and come and pray to me, and I will hear you. You will seek me and find me, when you seek me with all your heart. I will be found by you, declares the LORD, and I will restore your fortunes and gather you from all the nations and all the places where I have driven you, declares the LORD, and I will bring you back to the place from which I sent you into exile."*

Biblical error: This is also one of the flagship passages of the Health & Wealth crowd discussed earlier. It has commonly been misunderstood, and many preachers know this but use it anyway to encourage individualistic dreams for one's life.

Correcting the error: This passage gives no support to individualistic dreams, let alone dreams purported to come true in our lifetime. The passage very clearly refers to God's plans to restore the Judean exiles in the future (relative to the time Jeremiah was delivering God's message of hope). God is not promising prosperity to every believer for all time to come. Interpretations that offer up promises of individual prosperity and personal (often financial) hope often lead to people distrusting God or the Bible should they not prosper as they believed was promised (though God makes no such promise in this passage!) The reason that this passage is so often misinterpreted is that many people ignore its immediate context. A simple reading of the passage in context makes it clear to whom God's plans refer and why he would tell them this through his prophet Jeremiah.

Romans 8:28

> *And we know that in all things God works for the good of those who love him, who have been called according to his purpose.*

Biblical error: This verse is taught as a promise that God will make everything go our way.

Correcting the error: Romans 8:28 is not a promise that in the end we will get our dream job (or dream girl, dream house, etc.). It means that all things work together for character formation through suffering. Read the verse in its context! Providence is not the same as destiny. There can be more than one right choice when it comes to life decisions such as where to live, whom to marry, or what career to pursue. God works through even our own poor choices to help us continue to grow.

Range

This teaching is pervasive among evangelical and most charismatic churches (even among our own group in the churches of Christ).

Impact

Belief in having a specific and personal vision for one's life (as a divine mandate, not just sound life planning) can foster unhealthy anxiety about the future and an unhealthy reliance on those who claim they can help you "realize" your dreams. Maturity means total ownership of decisions; it is hard to do that when there's only one correct choice. Regret occurs when things go wrong; we may feel trapped. ("I would quit, but I need this job." "But now I'm married to him.")

In addition, the Visions and Dreams doctrine feeds narcissism. Another effect is that it can result in poor coping skills in the face of ambiguity or suffering. Yet another effect, especially on younger believers, is to cause them to feel they are (or must be) divinely called to full-time church work, when in truth, relatively few continue along this trajectory.

This doctrine has more in common in modern times with Western business culture, which trains executives to have a vision, a mission, and goals and objectives, and that achieving the goals and objectives in service of the mission will allow them to live up to the vision. Another source for some of the concepts embedded in this doctrine is the body of autosuggestion techniques encapsulated and expressed by the positive thinking and related movements.

Conclusion

There's nothing wrong with having a vision for your life and personal goals that help propel you forward. And if you focus on God's kingdom life (Matthew 5–7) and on doing what is right, then you can be confident that you will ultimately fulfill whatever vision God may have for you. Trust in God. Let him determine your steps and you will not fall. Remember Proverbs 16:9 (ESV): "The heart of man plans his way, but the Lord establishes his steps."

The next chapter is presented to afford perspective on a relatively modern doctrinal innovation, the Sinner's Prayer.

12

Bow & Pray – The New-Fangled Doctrine of 1835

Ask a Bible believer how one becomes a Christian, and chances are good (about 99%) they will say that you need to "receive Christ." This usually takes the form of some sort of prayer inviting Jesus into your heart. We both were taught this doctrine in our teen years.[11] But is this biblical—is it apostolic? That is, did Jesus instruct his disciples to proclaim the good news and call for a response of prayer? Is "receiving Christ" this way the historic teaching of the Christian church? Is there any example of this way of becoming a Christian before 1835, when it was first propagated in the United States?[12]

What This Movement Teaches

To become a Christian (saved), all that is necessary is to bow one's head and utter a sincere prayer asking the Lord Jesus to come into one's heart. This doctrine sometimes appears as the Sinner's Prayer, the Roman Road, or the Four Spiritual Laws.

Background

During the Protestant Reformation in the sixteenth century, the reformer Huldrych Zwingli was the first to maintain that the sacraments, including the Lord's Supper and baptism, rather than enacting and initiating that which they also symbolized, as had been believed from the times of the early Christians, instead were merely "outward signs of an inward grace" that did not actually do anything except point toward faith. Before this time, baptism was viewed as the "new birth" (John 3) into the life of Christ (Romans 6), in the context of which the believer's sins were forgiven and they received the Holy Spirit (Acts 2:36–41). The Lord's Supper was seen as unifying the body of Christ (the church) and fostering and deepening the believer's relationship with Christ on an ongoing basis.

During the Great Awakening in England and America, preachers addressing many thousands of people at a time focused on fostering emotional sorrow, which could be relieved by accepting or receiving Jesus into one's heart, an inference drawn from misinterpretations of Revelation 3:20 and John 1:12. This style of preaching was favored by many of the great evangelists and preachers of the eighteenth through twentieth centuries, who spoke to large crowds all over the world. The swift growth that resulted from such preaching swiftly popularized Bow and

Pray doctrines to the point that most evangelicals believe this is the normative means of being saved, even against the official teachings of many of their own denominations.

The Actual Biblical Emphasis

God responds to humble prayer. He wants to take up residence in our hearts. Conversion does not have to be a lengthy or complex process, yet it always involves a repentant sinner being saved by grace through faith as expressed in baptism into Christ and an ongoing life of obediently following Jesus and his teachings (Matthew 28:18–20; Mark 16:16; Acts 2:36–47; Romans 6:3–4; Ephesians 2:8–10; 4:4–6; 1 Peter 3:21).

Favored Biblical Texts

Revelation 3:20

Here I am! I stand at the door and knock. If anyone hears my voice and opens the door, I will come in and eat with that person, and they with me.

Biblical error: Overly zealous preachers from the time of the Great Awakening until the present day have misapplied this passage to non-Christian sinners in need of salvation, instead of rightly applying it to saved, Christian sinners in need of repentance.

Correcting the error: This is not even a conversion

passage at all. Jesus speaks to Christians here, not to non-Christians. The church is warned to repent (v.19), thus re-inviting Jesus into their hearts. In context, the passage is addressed to the members of the church in Laodicea (Revelation 3:14, see also 3:22).

John 1:12

Yet to all who did receive him, to those who believed in his name, he gave the right to become children of God

Biblical error: This verse is taught as describing the means of salvation.

Correcting the error: Receiving (accepting) Christ in John 1 is coming to terms with who he is. Those who accept the truth about him are not children of God; they merely have the right to *become* children of God (see also John 12:47–48). The new birth is not explained by the author until John 3 when Jesus tells the Pharisee Nicodemus that unless one is born again of water and the Spirit, one cannot enter the kingdom of heaven. Some teach that Jesus was not referring to baptism in John 3 but to human physical birth contrasted with the spiritual new birth. Yet this cannot be what is meant, since Jesus strongly corrected this very misunderstanding made by Nicodemus! (John 3:3–5). The universal understanding of this passage until recently was that it referred to baptism.

Ephesians 2:8–9 ESV

For by grace you have been saved through faith. And this is not your own doing; it is the gift of God, not a result of works, so that no one may boast.

Biblical error: These verses are often interpreted to mean that good works such as baptism cannot save a person.

Correcting the error: It is true that there is nothing we can do to earn our salvation and that good works are the result and expression of saving faith. However, baptism is not a "good work" of man as it is often supposed and presented. Baptism is the work of Christ, as explained in Colossians 2:8–15. Ironically, Paul warns his readers in Colossae not to be carried away by human traditions that teach the opposite.

Later in Ephesians, Paul will summarize the basis of Christian unity as being that there is "one body and one Spirit—just as you were called to the one hope that belongs to your call—one Lord, one faith, one baptism, one God and Father of all, who is over all and through all and in all" (Ephesians 4:4–6 ESV). This scripture became the basis for the earliest summary of the Christian faith known as the Rule of Faith. It was later expanded to become the core of the great creeds of Christendom such as the Apostles' Creed and the Nicene Creed, all of which contain the same basic elements as Ephesians 4:4–6.

The great reformer Martin Luther himself believed and taught that baptism led to salvation. In his Small (or Little) Catechism, he wrote that baptism "works forgiveness of sins, rescues from death and the devil, and gives eternal salvation to all who believe this, as the words and promises of God declare." Luther's Small Catechism briefly and clearly answers and corrects a lot of the false things that many modern Protestants believe about baptism. The catechism does this through reference directly to scriptures illustrating and summarizing the New Testament teaching about baptism.

Colossians 2:6

So then, just as you received Christ Jesus as Lord, continue to live your lives in him.

Biblical error: This verse is used as a conversion scripture, yet *how* one receives Jesus as Lord is not addressed.

Correcting the error: Colossians 2:6 speaks of the broader conversion process, not a prayer for salvation. There is not a single biblical example of someone becoming a Christian through the Bow-and-Pray method. Actually, baptism is the *true* "sinner's prayer" of the New Testament. All the conversions described in any detail in the New Testament after the ascension of Christ feature people responding to the proclamation of the gospel with a confession of faith and repentance and being baptized into Jesus (see the book of Acts).

Range

This doctrine is nearly universal among evangelicals, even among those whose denominations officially teach otherwise.

Impact

Millions of persons who have never repented (Acts 2:38; 3:19; 26:18) believe they have eternal life, merely by virtue of having bowed and prayed. The gospel message is diluted, and baptism and discipleship usually end up becoming optional.

Bow and Pray unwittingly encourages those coming to faith to do the bare minimum. They are asked to give mental assent to the fact that Jesus is Lord, instead of *following* him as Lord. Further, they are offered salvation from the consequences of sin (guilt and hell), instead of salvation from sin—which means the power to give up sin and live a holy life.

Conclusion

Study the Bible carefully, especially the teachings of Jesus and the Acts of the Apostles, to see what Jesus taught about salvation and what the apostles preached—

as well as how the earliest believers became Christians. Try to look past any preconceived notions of what they did and focus on what they really did. You will not find the modern and very popular notion of simply saying a prayer and receiving Jesus into one's heart.[13] Instead, you will see sinners who come to believe in Jesus deciding to repent—to change the orientation of their hearts and minds—and be baptized, receiving the gift of the Holy Spirit and persevering in living changed lives as followers of Jesus.

The final issue we address isn't so much a specific doctrine as a widespread human tendency: to add to the gospel.

13

Gospel Plus – When Guidelines Undermine Scripture

We may be critical of the Pharisees (Matthew 15; 23) and the Circumcision Party (Titus 1; see Acts 15), and rightly so, but what about us? Have we added to the demands and commands of Scripture? Before analyzing the Gospel+ beliefs, let's identify two varieties of legalism:

- *Type 1 Legalism:* This form of legalism attempts to power one's way into God's grace through good works. These works don't necessarily mean requirements outside Scripture. This may entail an unhealthy attitude toward obedience and acceptance by God, usually accompanied by anxiety over one's spiritual status before God.

- *Type 2 Legalism:* Following or enforcing extrabiblical rules—laws that, however well intended, are not explicitly found in Scripture (*extra,* Latin = outside; extrabiblical = outside Scripture). Examples of this include things such as establishing and enforcing evangelistic quotas, insistence on perfect living or perfect understanding before baptism, mandated minutes of prayer, and compulsory attendance at various church events. These may be good things, in principle. We appreciate evangelism, knowledge, prayer, devotional strategy, and church attendance. The question is, what does the gospel require?

What This Belief Teaches

Gospel+ comes in two flavors:

- *Hard version:* We cannot be saved before overcoming sin and beginning to live as a disciple. These changes can and must be brought about *before* one possesses the indwelling gift of the Holy Spirit. After conversion, the standard must be upheld to retain salvation.
- *Soft version:* Although we are saved by grace, we stay saved and/or we mature only by following extrabiblical rules.

The Actual Biblical Emphasis

Obedience to God's word is paramount. We *should* be willing to go to great lengths to keep our hearts engaged in the Lord's work. Local churches have a responsibility to provide leadership and guidance.

Favored Biblical Texts

Luke 14:33

> *In the same way, those of you who do not give up everything you have cannot be my disciples.*

Biblical error: It is taught that this verse gives leaders the right to mandate specific sacrifices.

Correcting the error: "Giving up everything" is not unlimited, but should be interpreted in the light of apostolic teaching, as found in the epistles and in Acts. In addition, it is up to each individual in any given situation to decide whether and how to "give up" or sacrifice their time, money, relationships, opinions, and so forth as directed by their conscience, the Holy Spirit, and the teachings of Scripture.

Hebrews 13:7

> *Remember your leaders, who spoke the word of God to you. Consider the outcome of their way of life and imitate their faith.*

Biblical error: This verse is used to teach that leaders must be obeyed in all aspects, including matters of opinion.

Correcting the error: Leaders have authority, but not to

create their own rules (Deuteronomy 4:2; Proverbs 30:5–6; 1 Corinthians 4:6; Revelation 22:18–19). We mustn't fail to distinguish between *principle* and *practice* (that is, implementation). These rules may be called "guidelines," but one can tell whether they have been elevated to near-biblical status by the reaction when they are violated. Some fear the gospel by itself is too gracious and might tempt (or even empower) us to slack off. Yet grace is empowering, and those who don't experience it don't endure long in the marathon of faith.

Range

These beliefs are common to most biblically and morally conservative or fundamentalist groups, none of which has completely resisted the temptation to go beyond what is written.

Impact

Under both forms of Gospel+ legalism, spirituality—one's own and that of others'—is constantly monitored and evaluated by adherence to rules. This erodes the security and confidence we should have in the Lord (1 John 5:13; Matthew 11:28–30).

Conclusion:

Legalism in all its forms is often difficult to see

because it seems very reasonable and fits well with the way our worldly minds naturally work. The apostle Paul exhorts the believers:

> *For freedom Christ has set us free; stand firm therefore, and do not submit again to a yoke of slavery. Look: I, Paul, say to you that if you accept circumcision, Christ will be of no advantage to you. I testify again to every man who accepts circumcision that he is obligated to keep the whole law. You are severed from Christ, you who would be justified by the law; you have fallen away from grace. For through the Spirit, by faith, we ourselves eagerly wait for the hope of righteousness. For in Christ Jesus neither circumcision nor uncircumcision counts for anything, but only faith working through love* (Galatians 5:1–6 ESV).

Younger disciples often benefit from guidelines, yet even then these should be a matter of consent, not law.

Every church inevitably needs some "rules" (not necessarily bad), like "Church starts at 9:00," or "Members need to participate in a small group." Still, these do not have divine authority. There may be exceptions, and churches should allow for some flexibility in implementation.

Our parting words (in Chapter 14) are important. We

would be horrified if our book became a cause of disunity. With this concern in mind, we ask you to hear us out as we close with a caution, a challenge, and a plea.

14

Caution, Challenge & Plea

Informed may not have been what you were expecting. Perhaps to some, we may have seemed too strict—too critical. To others, we may have been too flexible—too "liberal." We are aware of the potential perils involved in encouraging others to think for themselves. In situations where biblical instruction has been absent, or spiritual maturity lacking, information can easily go to one's head. It can hurt others (1 Corinthians 8:1, 11), especially when only partially digested. We want to encourage you, as we did at the beginning of the book, to think for yourself including about the things in this book. We do not exempt our own material from the need for scrutiny, criticism, and feedback. We don't demand that you agree with everything you have read, but we do expect that you have been thinking, asking questions, evaluating, checking, and confirming or disconfirming anything about which you have doubts or questions.

In the spirit of our opening chapter, we would like to leave you with three things: a caution, a challenge, and a plea.

The Caution

As funny as it may sound, as seekers of truth, we need to take care not to be *too* openminded. There is a difference between being receptive and being naïve. Solomon grasped the distinction. "The simple believe anything, but the prudent give thought to their steps" (Proverbs 14:15). When we are naively credulous, we lose credibility.

Also apropos is Chesterton's insight: "An open mind is like an open mouth: its purpose is to bite on something nourishing. Otherwise, it becomes like a sewer, accepting everything, rejecting nothing."[14] Or, moving from an urban illustration to a more rural one: "An open mind, like an open window, should be equipped with a screen to keep the bugs out."[15]

There are several things that can make us "too" open—overly receptive to false teaching:

- Immature attraction to novelty (Hebrews 13:8–9)
- Pride—desire to have access to special knowledge, or be "in the know" (Proverbs 18:2)
- Worldliness—thinking influenced by unbiblical or humanistic notions (Romans 12:2; Ephesians 4:20–24).
- Unresolved feelings about church or church leadership (Hebrews 12:15)

- A desire to rationalize sin through a lowered standard of commitment to the Lord (2 Peter 2:10; Numbers 16:1–2)
- Idol worship of our favorite teachers or authors, leading to uncritical processing of their talks, books, podcasts, etc.

Let's be curious—but cautious. Let's not overestimate our own insight or objectivity (Romans 12:3). Weigh new ideas (1 Thessalonians 5:21). Evaluate unfamiliar scriptural interpretations by reading passages in context. Seek input from mature believers. Take time to think—and rethink.

The Challenge

Jesus taught us to build on the rock—to base our lives on his teachings, embracing his word without compromise. Consider his instruction at the end of the Sermon on the Mount:

> *"Enter through the narrow gate. For wide is the gate and broad is the road that leads to destruction, and many enter through it. But small is the gate and narrow the road that leads to life, and only a few find it.*
>
> *"Watch out for false prophets. They come to you in sheep's clothing, but inwardly they are ferocious wolves. By their fruit you will recognize them...*

> *"Not everyone who says to me, 'Lord, Lord,' will enter the kingdom of heaven, but only the one who does the will of my Father who is in heaven. Many will say to me on that day, 'Lord, Lord, did we not prophesy in your name and in your name drive out demons and in your name perform many miracles?' Then I will tell them plainly, 'I never knew you. Away from me, you evildoers!'*
>
> *"Therefore everyone who hears these words of mine and puts them into practice is like a wise man who built his house on the rock. The rain came down, the streams rose, and the winds blew and beat against that house; yet it did not fall, because it had its foundation on the rock. But everyone who hears these words of mine and does not put them into practice is like a foolish man who built his house on sand. The rain came down, the streams rose, and the winds blew and beat against that house, and it fell with a great crash"* (Matthew 7:13–16a, 21–27).

What are the dangers of which Christ warns us—pitfalls for "shepherds" and "sheep" alike?

- The broad road, which can often be more appealing than the narrow road and is easier to preach (7:13–14)
- Desire for influence and an attraction to false teachers (7:15)

- Bearing bad fruit (7:16–20)
- "Talk" without "walk"—which is disobedience to the will of the Father (7:21)
- Placing excessive confidence in spiritual experiences (7:22)
- A false relationship with Christ because of a lack of biblical love for God (7:23)[16]
- Building on "sand" (7:24–27); it is quicker to take shortcuts, but it means we are at greater risk when the storms come

Building on the Word is a continuous process, not a one-time event. This means ongoing training is essential for *anyone* who wants to read the Bible well. Let's hold ourselves to a high standard. And let's hold every Christian teacher or leader accountable, too.[17] Training, study, and learning are not only for those respected as academics or "teachers" of the faith, since *all* church leaders must be "able to teach" (1 Timothy 3:2; Titus 1:9).

If you are a church leader, what is your ongoing plan for continuing education? Are you actively learning from others—including those outside your church family? And if we have been Christians for a while, how is our appetite for Scripture? (Matthew 4:4; Hebrews 5:11–14; 1 Peter 2:2).

The Plea

Biblical knowledge is essential. Jesus lambasted the religious leadership of his day on their faulty knowledge of Scripture (Matthew 22:29). The content of our message is more significant than the style in which it is delivered. Doctrine matters. However, it is a sad legacy of many conservative churches that doctrine has been used as a weapon. Those whose interpretation of a text may differ from our own are sometimes labeled as false teachers. Yet these are not always the "wolves" of Matthew 7. In fact, sometimes their commitment to the Lord puts us to shame.

It is too easy to treat every doctrine and tradition as black and white—to ignore the gray. Some people make blanket statements like "All commands are equally important," or "All sins are equally serious." Yet the topography of the Bible is not flat; there are peaks, ridges, and canyons—some things are more significant than others (Matthew 22:35–40; 23:23). Imagining that they themselves have mastered the Bible, some who are overconfident regard with suspicion any differing viewpoint. "Anyone who teaches a falsehood is a false teacher." Such attitudes serve to bolster control, to put distance between believers, and to build walls. (Fences are much more friendly.) Notice that in this book, we do not attack false teachers, rather we examine false beliefs, misinterpretations, and faulty understanding.

Knowledge is not to be used as a bludgeon. First, because that is ungracious. Second, because we may be mistaken. We all change our minds occasionally, indicating we *were* wrong—though hopefully are now moving toward a more mature understanding of the Word. Too often we have heard 1 Corinthians 1:10 misused. "I appeal to you… that all of you agree with one another in what you say and that there be no divisions among you, but that you be perfectly united in mind and thought." The unity of which Paul writes is not total agreement on every point of Scripture, but rather on core teachings (e.g., 1 Corinthians 15:1–4). The disunity at Corinth sometimes did have doctrinal roots, but worldliness and ego were the deeper issues (1 Corinthians 3:3; 3:1–22; 6:7; 13:11). Moreover, Paul did not insist that everyone think identically—only that they preserve Christian unity. Unity is not uniformity.[18]

On the contrary; Christian unity *depends* on diversity! (1 Corinthians 12:4–13:8a). I (Joseph, in this case) come from a very diverse ethnic heritage. The motto of one of the countries of my roots is "Out of Many, One People," referring to the multiethnic and multiracial "pot o' mixup" (which means something similar to the metaphor of a cultural "melting pot") heritage of the people, the food, the language, and the culture. Similarly, the church is the unification of Jew and Gentile (Ephesians 2), of followers of Jesus from every nation (Matthew 28:16–20), and of an entire world united and made new in Christ (Romans 8:18–25). Our common culture is no longer national or ethnic, but spiritual (and I don't mean "church culture"!). Our common culture is defined by the life and teachings of Christ himself. It is a culture that should be, above all, characterized by love (John 13:34–35; 1 Corinthians 13).

The more traditions, guidelines, and rules we lay down—going beyond what is written (1 Corinthians 4:6; Proverbs 30:5–6)—the less our chances of unity. Those who differ on various matters of interpretation become the enemy. Anxiety levels escalate. Harsh judgments follow, and severe disciplines may be meted out.

Several centuries ago, a wise man observed, "It would be strange indeed [that] the church should require more than Christ himself did, or make other conditions of her communion than our Savior did of discipleship… Without all controversy, the main inlet of all the distractions, confusion, and divisions of the Christian world hath been adding of other conditions of church-communion than Christ hath done."[19] Or, more succinctly, "In essentials, unity; in nonessentials, liberty; in all things, charity."[20]

Theological depth and sensitivity to nuance require significant periods of reflection. This is as true for others as it is for you and me. Are we patient with those who need more time to process certain biblical teachings? Consider Paul's admonition:

> *All of us, then, who are mature should take such a view of things. And if on some point you think differently, that too God will make clear to you. Only let us live up to what we have already attained* (Philippians 3:15–16).

Since, as Paul points out, none of us has arrived—we are all en route to the destination—a crucial question must be asked. Is there grace for doctrinal shortcomings? We are generally quick to think the best of those who repent of moral failings. We allow them time to change. We certainly don't demand instant moral perfection. Usually, we are happy with noticeable progress (Philippians 1:25). If there is grace for moral failings, might there also be grace for doctrinal failings?

As we discussed in Chapter 1, sound doctrine concerns our walk—our spiritual life—more than the technical angles of theology, anyway. Try to answer the following question honestly:

> At the Judgment, would I rather have lived a sincere and Christ-centered life—though with an incomplete understanding of theology, or hold a perfect understanding of correct doctrine—yet with a life carelessly out of line with God's will?

As one theologian put it, "I don't believe that God is a fussy faultfinder in dealing with theological ideas. He who provides forgiveness for a sinful life will also surely be a generous judge of theological reflections."[21] Is this a dangerous idea? Perhaps. Yet doesn't this viewpoint better match the spirit and teachings of our Lord (e.g., Matthew 7:1–5) than a strict, sectarian stance?

Summary

Before we say adieu, we reiterate our caution, challenge, and plea. While revering the Lord and his word (Psalm 138:2),

- *Caution:* Let's keep our minds open—but not recklessly so.
- *Challenge:* Let's study, learn, and build on God's word—on an ongoing basis.
- *Plea:* Let's aim to embody God's grace toward others—just as we remain in his grace.

Notes

1. Andy Olsen, "The church's complex relationship with the classics," ***Christianity Today*** (Carol Stream, IL), September 2019, 7.

2. Every group has boundaries. Unless we can determine who is inside the group and who is outside, it will prove difficult to shepherd them. It is true that theological misconceptions sometimes cause great harm. But it is ungodly living that is the clearer and more present danger. It is tempting to erect a system of creeds and rules—those things a church member in good standing must agree on, and what policies they must adhere to.

3. Bible teachers sometimes turn to 1 Timothy 4:16 to affirm that right doctrine is just as important as right living. Sometimes we teachers asked, "Which wing of the airplane is more important, the left or the right?" That is a fair question, especially if we understand life and doctrine in the way Paul wrote to Timothy. Yet the passage is misapplied when we fail to use the word "doctrine" as it has been explained in Paul's letters.

4. For even more material, see Douglas Jacoby, ***Till the Nets Are Full: An Evangelism Handbook for the 21st Century*** (Spring, TX: Illumination Publishing, 2018).

5. Dallas Willard, ***The Divine Conspiracy: Rediscovering Our Hidden Life in God*** (New York, NY: HarperSanFrancisco, 1998), 275. The words of the quotation in the ellipsis: "We can see that it is not doctrinal correctness because many people who cannot even understand the correct doctrines nevertheless place their full faith in him. Moreover, we find many people who seem to be very correct doctrinally but have hearts full of hatred and unforgiveness."

6. For a consideration of how terminology affects how we think and act, see https://www.douglasjacoby.com/terminology-reinforces-theology/.

7. Further: When I (Joey) first discovered Jeremiah 29:11–14, I was keen to use it to help believers to seek God. "Hope and a future" is just what they want and need, I thought. How wonderful that God plans to prosper us—that life will be better if we put him first! This is true, yet many readers today go well beyond the meaning of the passage, in the belief that God has a personalized plan, specifically designed for the happiness of each believer. This is simply not true—at least I've never found a scriptural passage that supports it. Many believers take Jeremiah 29 to guarantee a quick blessing—part of our on-demand culture? But the Lord says the blessing may take generations to be fulfilled. We shouldn't stand around waiting for the blessing to come; we should get on with life and faithfully persevere. (Read the chapter in its entirety, and you may confirm that modern evangelicals have woefully misread this great passage.)

8. Thomas à Kempis, ***The Imitation of Christ,*** Book 2, chapter 11.

9. For a short paper on the events surrounding the destruction of Jerusalem, see https://www.douglasjacoby.com/wp-content/uploads/2003/12/DJer80.pdf.
10. Miroslav Volf, "Human Flourishing" in ***Renewing the Evangelical Mission,*** ed. Richard Lints (Grand Rapids, MI: Eerdmans, 2013).
11. Douglas was sixteen and Joseph thirteen when they were asked to say the Sinner's Prayer.
12. For the history of the roots of the Sinner's Prayer, you may want to read Stephen Staten's helpful article, https://www.douglasjacoby.com/the-sinner-s-prayer/.
13. For a telling admission of the paucity of evidence for the new-fangled doctrine of 1835, take a look at the satirical article "Bible Lacking Sinner's Prayer Returned for Full Refund," Babylon Bee, August 16, 2016, http://babylonbee.com/news/bible-lacking-sinners-prayer-returned-full-refund/.
14. G.K. Chesterton, ***The Collected Works of G.K. Chesterton*** (San Francisco, CA: Ignatius, 1986), 16:212.
15. Virginia Hutchinson, https://bustedhalo.com/dailyjolt/lent-2011-april-18.
16. See John 14:23–24 and Deuteronomy 7:8–9. Further, as Paul explains, "Whoever loves God is known by God" (1 Corinthians 8:3). In other words, if Jesus never knew us, it is because we did not properly love him.
17. Consider also the important Old Testament text Deuteronomy 17:18–20.

18. See www.douglasjacoby.com/unity-on-three-levels-2005/.
19. Edward Stillingfleet, Dean of St Paul's London, 1659.
20. Peter Meiderlin (Rupertus Meldenius), Lutheran theologian, 1626.
21. Helmut Thielicke, ***A Little Exercise for Young Theologians,*** tr. Charles L. Taylor (Grand Rapids, MI: Eerdmans, 1962), 37.